Presented to
    Helen Caldwell
June 5, 1983
for 3 years of perfect
attendance at
Hickory U.P. Church School

Grace
Abounding

Grace Abounding

Gordon C. Hunter

ABINGDON   Nashville

GRACE ABOUNDING

Library of Congress Cataloging in Publication Data

HUNTER, GORDON C
  1. Christian life—1960- 2. Grace
(Theology) I. Title.
BV4501.2.H829   248'.4   77-21326

ISBN 0-687-15679-3

Manufactured by the Parthenon Press at
Nashville, Tennessee, United States of America

"For the grace of God has dawned upon the world with healing for all mankind."
—*Titus 2:11 NEB*

Preface

When I asked my mentor in Christ, Dr. E. Stanley Jones, to write a preface to my chapters on grace, he enthusiastically consented to do so. However, illness and then his passing precluded that possibility. He has expressed his thoughts on the subject of grace in several of his books.

> *The Way is the way of grace.* . . . The Gospel starts . . . with grace. It is God's initiative that redeems us. Deissman says: "All the religions of the world begin with man's initiative—man searching for God. In Christianity God takes the initiative." . . . I once listened to an address in India by a visiting lecturer on "Man's search for God," and at the close a Scotch missionary quietly said, "Have you read *The Hound of Heaven?* If not, go sell your coat and buy it." *The Hound of Heaven* depicts the Love of God pursuing us down the years. . . . We do not find God, we put ourselves in the way of being found by God.
>
> [The Gospel] is not primarily a teaching us how to live, but an offer of Life. Jesus did not come to show us the Way, but to show Himself as the Way. "He did not come to preach the Gospel, but that there might be a Gospel to be preached." . . .
>
> Grace is everywhere, healing, redeeming, saving. "Where sin abounded grace did much more abound." "The grace of . . . Jesus Christ overflowed far more richly." (Rom. 5:15, Moffatt.) . . .
>
> Grace is free, but when once you take it you are bound forever to the Giver. . . .
>
> Grace strengthens you. "Be strong in the grace of Christ Jesus." (II Tim. 2:1, Moffatt.) . . .

.

When you start with grace, then everything is open to you. Life is one glad, glorious, opening surprise. (*The Way* [Abingdon, 1946], pp. 190, 195, 196)

Again, Stanley Jones writes:

Perhaps the most distinctive thing in the gospel is grace, so the most distinctive thing in our growth must be growth in grace. The grace of God is love judging our sins, suffering for our sins, forgiving our sins, removing our sins, and then abiding in unworthy hearts. That is grace. (*Victorious Living* [Abingdon, 1936], p. 333)

Again:

The central thing in Christ Jesus is grace. "Grace and truth came through Jesus Christ." He was full of grace and truth. Others brought truth but no grace. Others still brought grace but no truth. The two came together in Him—His grace was truthful; His truth was gracious. Grace can be defined verbally as unmerited favor, but vitally grace can only be defined as Jesus. There we see grace—the Word of grace become flesh. Looking at Him as grace we see the most beautiful thing ever seen on our planet. Grace is love with open arms. Grace is love with tears upon its cheeks saying, "Come home."

This grace is "immeasurable." . . . There are no limits; no matter what you have done, or have been, no matter what you are, grace has open arms, gives you a new start, opens the door to boundless development. (*In Christ* [Abingdon, 1961], p. 236)

So, I believe that if he had written this Preface independently of his books, he would have said much the same as I have quoted. I am grateful for his words and for so much else that I learned from him about living the abundant life. These quotations provide an appropriate opening for the theme of this book.

Contents

Introduction

In between sessions of the conference at which I was sharing leadership, I decided to go for a brisk walk. Fresh air and exercise were not built in to the event; so I had to seek them on my own.

What a magnificent winter day in northern Ontario! Clear blue sky, bracing cold air, white snow everywhere. I inhaled deeply, stepped lively, and praised God. Then, without warning, there came over me a few moments of total ecstasy. "Everything was beautiful," as the song says. I was overwhelmed by an inner experience of exhilaration in simply being alive. Then my mind suddenly cleared. Scintillating thoughts and surprising insights began to tumble into my thinking. At first I longed for paper and pen to get them down, because I knew these clear thoughts wouldn't last. But then I felt this to be one of those extremely rare moments in life that must not be intruded upon. Even the simple process of writing would break the spell.

As I continued, the crisp snow crunching under my feet, it came to me to give names to my legs. One I called "grace," and the other gratitude." I began repeating those words as I walked: grace and gratitude, grace and gratitude.

Suddenly it struck me that here was the essential rhythm of the Christian life. We accept grace and respond in gratitude. God takes the initiative and we receive. Our life in Christ is always a *responsive* life. God is giver, prompter, initiator. We answer with gratitude, faith, love, and service.

Just as quickly as it had come, the experience passed. A rumbling truck and a barking dog brought me back to earth. But the experience will remain forever in my memory and continue to inspire and challenge me. I believe such moments are direction points. Some may question whether times like these are an escape from reality or a leap into the very center of reality. I am convinced that the latter is the truth. Occasionally in life we have times when the veil of this world is temporarily removed, when we see past ordinary objects and perceive a world of truth normally unknown. A vision? Call it what you like. It is a time when the deeper consciousness takes over, and we feel enveloped, filled, expanded.

What remains of this is the certainty that the first and most important step is to receive God's gifts. Grace must come before gratitude. Without accepting what God has to give, there is no rationale for making response.

Pondering this, I have often asked myself what would happen if I began each day by saying, "Father, what gifts do you have for me today?" In fact, many times I have found myself doing just that. I get out of bed looking for, being sensitive to, and consciously accepting God's gifts. How fantastically it transforms my day! It heightens my sensitivity to what is going on. Instead of fighting life, I find myself embracing it, including the difficulties as well as the good things. I have learned that many of God's good gifts are hidden in those experiences I most often resist and try to fend off. In every difficult task there is a gift wrapped in a blessing. Countless people discovered this long before myself and, like Helen Keller, have come to thank God even for their disabilities because through those they have found themselves, their vocation, and their God.

But then the thought: Could this be just a subtle form of selfishness? Does it make our relationship to God only a one-way street? I believe not. Mind you, this could be the case if the whole business stopped this side of our response in terms of gratitude, love, and service. But gratitude immediately shifts the emphasis from self to God and makes us adventurers in discovering ways and means of expressing that gratitude in loving attitudes and meaningful service.

This makes living exciting. Some days we may just move out into our regular responsibilities not having received any specific gift but convinced there are gifts waiting for us. We then discover that they come as God's surprises. While not consciously looking for them or making any specific request, we become sensitized to their appearing. Then we may say in our new awareness, "That's a gift. I'll take it and use it." With some practice this can become a way of life.

I remember standing with a small group of people in a circle of thanksgiving. It marked the end of a weekend we had spent together during which we had taken an honest inventory of ourselves and discovered new ways of becoming whole persons. One man spoke up: "I'm grateful that God has shown me how ungrateful I really am. It's either gratitude or resentment, and I've sure had my share of resentment. I want to change!"

That's what this book is all about. Many people are beating their heads against stone walls trying to get something out of life. The gambling craze indicates that multitudes want something more of life than what is now their fare (and for nothing if they can only get their hands on that magic number). But this turns out to be a futile business because it misses God's gifts of grace and, win or lose, results in a cynical view of the way things are.

Some may say of grace, "I'll believe it when I see it." I would answer, "Open your eyes." God's initiative is everywhere, but only as we are open to him to receive his gifts can we experience this divine flow toward us. You may want to call this faith, and that's OK. But I believe that just being aware of grace *is* grace. Start from there. It's a simple beginning with no ending, for we are soon deluged by evidences of God's outpouring love.

So in these pages we will explore a few of the meanings of grace and ways of responding to it.

This book is gratefully dedicated to the memory of my father, Dr. E. Crossley Hunter, whose fruitful ministry, in The Methodist Church in Canada and then the United Church of Canada, spanned more than fifty years.

The Privilege of Living

Have you ever thought of life as being a privilege? I hadn't until I came across an old story that has had a profound influence on me over many years.

There were two men in a business partnership. One night, just as they were locking up and preparing to go home, they stopped to greet an elderly man who operated a store next to theirs. One of them spoke up.

"Just a moment while I ask you a question. I've often wondered what keeps you going. Here you are twice our age. You arrive early in the morning. You have a busy day. But I notice that every night you are just like a schoolboy getting out when the school bell rings. How is it you appear full of vitality when we're so tired? What's your secret?"

"Oh," he replied, "I don't think I have any particular secret. But over the years I've discovered this one thing: *"a man's spirit"* never gets tired so long as he is heartily grateful for the privilege of living."

When I first read that last phrase, it caught and held my imagination and has become a key to opening a whole new way of life for me. I've concluded that most people could be classified into one of two basic types: those who are fighting for their rights or those who are realizing their privileges. The first group feels cheated, convinced they are getting much less out of life than they deserve or desire. But the second feels so deluged with good things that even a very long life would not allow sufficient time to express in either words or actions their overflowing gratitude. The first group tends to be cynical and sickly, the second healthy and happy.

A teen-aged girl wrote "I'm Glad I Had Polio." I could hardly believe my eyes when I read that title. How could anybody say that? She tells how she was selfish, proud, and greedy until polio struck. For weeks she lay in her hospital bed unable to move. Then one day to her amazement she discovered she could wiggle one toe, just enough to notice. She says of that experience, "My heart ached from too much gratitude." From that tiny beginning, strength came slowly into her limbs, and through it all, she says, "I learned the privilege of health." Perhaps this is not so much a key as a law. And wherever and whenever it is applied it changes everything. For instance, the Ontario Department of Highways published a booklet on safe driving. At the bottom of the center spread were the words: "Remember, to drive a car is not a right but a privilege." I thought about that; most accidents are caused by irresponsibility or carelessness. Merely to have a license doesn't give the right to drive but rather the privilege to drive. If more people had this attitude, they would drive with a greater sense of responsibility, and the accident rate would go down.

So here is something that can be universally applied, and it works the same benefits toward citizenship, education, daily work, friendship. A sense of privilege leads to deeper gratitude which, in turn, issues in greater responsibility.

The Bible reflects this attitude. "My cup runs over" (Ps. 23:5 NEB). "The lines are fallen unto me in pleasant places; . . . I have a goodly heritage" (Ps. 16:6). I would have lost heart if I had not seen "the goodness of the Lord in the land of the living" (Ps. 27:13 RSV). "The Lord has dealt bountifully with me" (Ps. 13:6 RSV). He loads me with benefits every day (see Ps. 68:19).

I am convinced that if once this approach to life really gets hold of us, a thousand things can change for the better. But how can that happen? One way to start is by remembering that life itself is a gift. Nobody is self-made, though there are many who take a lot of credit for themselves. Each heartbeat, each breath, each day, is a gift. These cannot be bought or deserved or created, only received. "It is he that made us" (Ps. 100:3 RSV).

Every new morning is a gift. Put your head on a pillow at night, and you can do nothing at all to make another day come. It cannot be bought or created or deserved or demanded. Should another day dawn for you, after the gift of sleep, then it will come as another gift.

I went to a hospital to visit a very sick man. He knew the seriousness of his condition and said to me, "Gordon, I'm living on borrowed time." I went away with those words turning in my mind. But as I opened my car door the thought struck me that I too am living on borrowed time, and so is everybody else. Days and seasons and years are gifts.

A man said, "Before I became a Christian for real, I used to resist living. I would force myself out of bed and say, 'Good Lord. It's morning.' Now, having learned to accept God's gifts, I say, 'Good morning, Lord.'" What a difference!

The world around us is a gift. We didn't create that either. I think of this whenever I reread the story of the garden of Eden. Adam and Eve walked around that place as if it were theirs by right, forgetting that it was God's gift for them to use. They had no rights, only privileges.

17

Forgetting that, they disobeyed, brought upon themselves the curse, and were driven out. It is precisely this kind of attitude that has brought on our current ecological crisis. We treat the earth as if it were ours to exploit. What food we throw away could feed whole populations among starving nations. Once again the psalms guide us here. "The earth is the Lord's and the fulness thereof" (24:1 RSV).

It's easy to slide into a way of indulgent thinking. A little girl asked her friend, "Does your daddy say grace at meals?"

"What do you mean?" the other girl replied.

"Well, before you eat doesn't he thank God for all the food on the table?"

"Why, no," she answered. "You see, my daddy doesn't have to thank God, because we own the grocery store."

What we buy, what we create, what we think we own, is only possible because of "original" gifts that only God or others can supply to us. We take these and rearrange them or build upon them so that something beautiful and satisfying will result.

The people of our family are gifts to us. Nobody can create another person, much as one may wish to re-create someone else with improvement in mind.

Love cannot be bought or demanded. It must be a gift of one person to another and, therefore, can only be received. This makes it a matter of grace, an undeserved blessing and, for those reasons, a privilege. The words *I love you* are beautiful, but the words *thank you for loving me* are more beautiful still.

A woman said, "Nobody works as hard for so little monetary return as a wife and mother in the home." A man listening to her said, "But when a woman marries, doesn't she promise to love, to honor, and no pay?"

Without exploiting this story, the truth remains that within the family nobody can be paid. If you start payment for services rendered, you no longer have a family; you have a business. When the prodigal son left for the far country, he demanded his "pay" and got it. But when he came home he had a new attitude, having become aware of his privileges. The family that is made up of people who love us when we're not lovable, who forgive us when we don't deserve it, who support us and boost us and affirm us when we've made a mess of things, who support our belief in ourselves and in our inner worth, is something that cannot be bought at any price. It is and must be a gift and therefore a privilege.

But look further still. What about the Christian life itself? Jesus said to his disciples, "You did not choose me, but I chose you" (John 15:16 RSV). He wanted to get this matter straight. Being a Christian is not so much our idea of doing something for God but, by accepting God's gift of grace, letting him do something wonderful for us and through us. John reflects this thought when he wrote, "We love, because he first loved us" (I John 4:19 RSV).

This matter of grace is the basis of all Christian thought and action. The whole business is started by receiving the Gift, God himself in Jesus Christ, and goes on as we continue to receive an endless flow of gifts. "Grace upon grace" (John 1:16 RSV), John describes it. New Testament references to this process could fill a book. Here are just a few: "God so loved the world that he *gave*" (John 3:16 RSV); "he *gave* power to become children of God" (John 1:12 RSV); "my peace I *give* to you" (John 14:27 RSV); "the good shepherd *giveth* his life for the sheep" (John 10:11); "ask, and it shall be *given* you" (Luke 11:9);

"it is your Father's good pleasure to *give* you the kingdom" (Luke 12:32); "for by grace you have been saved through faith; and this is not your own doing, it is the *gift* of God" (Eph. 2:8 RSV).

God doesn't come to me with oppressive demands but with gifts. Faith is a gift and so is love. Forgiveness is a gift and so is power. And he not only gives outright gifts but heightens every natural gift within. When I become aware of grace, I discover that my intelligence is sharpened, my will more highly motivated, my energy stimulated.

Perhaps this was the big lesson Peter learned in the Upper Room when Jesus proceeded to wash his disciples' feet. Peter looked on in confused bewilderment. He might have asked himself; "What's he doing now? Why this?"

Obviously something was wrong. Since Jesus is teacher and Lord, leader and Messiah, it would be right for one of them to wash his feet, then, at his request, to wash one another's feet. But to have him kneel down and perform this lowly job? "Never!" Peter said.

Then Jesus put it to him clearly. "If you don't allow me to do this for you, you and I can have no fellowship." It then dawned on Peter what the good news was all about, that it was a matter of accepting grace and receiving gifts. Then he swung to the opposite extreme with his request, "Lord, not just my feet but head and hands as well" (see John 13:1–9).

Well, I don't know what this may say to you. But to me it means a choice. Either I take the road typified by the existentialist philosopher Jean-Paul Sartre in his book *Nausea*, in which he says simply, "I exist and find it sickening." Or, I can listen to an alternate approach to life expressed by an anonymous poet:

What a privilege to be alive!
To awake each day as if our Maker's grace
Did us afresh from nothingness derive,
That we might sing—How happy is our case,
What a privilege it is
To be alive!

I've already made up my mind that the way of grace and privilege and gratitude is the more realistic way to live. It takes in more of the facts and reflects a more valid approach in addition to making life an exciting adventure. To me it is self-verifying. But I am discovering more and more the fantastic truth in what that old man said, "A man's spirit never gets tired so long as he is heartily grateful for the privilege of living."

Living Life as a Gift

In the last chapter I tried to make the point that life is a gift and that everything about life is a matter of receiving gifts. But how does this work out in practical ways for the person sincerely trying to make life count?

Christian living could be broken up into three main parts: worship, work, and witness. Yet many people find that each of these has its own built-in problems and frustrations.

Worship, for instance. We've just come through a long period in which the various denominations have been engaged in liturgical renewal. We've seen all kinds of innovations introduced into the worship experience mostly, I suppose, for the purpose of making it all more "relevant" as well as attractive. I say attractive because there has been a decided drop in church attendance practically everywhere, especially in mainline churches.

The religious news editor of Canada's largest daily newspaper, *The Toronto Star*, says that organized, institutional Christianity "is in serious trouble and disarray." He cites the dramatic plunge in church attendance. "Unless the trend is reversed," he writes, "Canadian churches are headed for the same kind of devastation that has already struck their counterparts in Great Britain and much of Europe." One church editor suggests that the time has come to issue a statement to rank and file, forthrightly insisting that it is a Christian obligation to attend worship regularly.

I doubt that will do much good. Forced worship is not real. To attend church out of a sense of duty or obligation is to set up an inner resistance to the benefits and blessings that are potentially there. On the other hand, to come into a familiar sanctuary which in itself lifts the heart, to meditate upon God and his purpose for life, to confess our sins and experience his forgiveness, to have our minds refreshed, our nerves steadied, our courage strengthened, and our hope quickened, plus all the other benefits of worship, physical as well as spiritual, is something that cannot be bought for any price. It's not duty. It's privilege.

The real question is not why more people do not attend worship but why so many do. To be sure, there are many who apparently get very little out of it. One woman said that the only thing she could remember of a service was that the usher's shoes squeaked. But contrast that to the man who lived in northern Saskatchewan and who walked to his local church one winter morning when the temperature was forty degrees below. Being the only one who arrived, he put on the fire in the old barrel stove and sat there by himself. Casually he picked up a hymnbook, and his eyes fell on these words:

> Love of God, so pure and changeless,
> Blood of Christ, so rich and free,
> Grace of God, so strong and boundless,—
> Magnify them all in me.
> —Elizabeth Codner

He thought about them, turned them over in his mind, considered his past, his current life-style, his problems, failures, needs. Silently he bowed his head and prayed. When he looked at his watch, to his surprise a full hour had passed. This led to his becoming a different man with a changed attitude and a new life direction.

Worship surrounds us with a hundred influences, any one of which could profoundly influence us, heal us, guide us, stabilize us, or make us new. What wealth is available in public worship! Not dependent on the sermon alone, it is a total experience resulting from architecture, pageantry, music, instruction, inspiration, fellowship, and much, much more. No wonder we sing "What a privilege, to carry/Everything to God in prayer." To look on worship in this way is to be open to its riches.

The same is true with church work. The structure of the church depends on multitudes of ordinary people who teach, administer, sit on committees, or visit. Unfortunately, for many it is a burden, a necessity (because there's no one else), or an attempt to be loyal to parental upbringing. But there is little that is inspiring, and their vitality soon runs down.

Following my ordination in 1948, my wife, Anna, and I headed for our first appointment in British Columbia. We found ourselves living and serving in the midst of the vast ranching territory of that magnificent province. The area is called "the Cariboo," and it has been considered Canada's last frontier. I was a traveling missionary.

No sooner had we arrived than we heard people talking about the "cattle sale." Asking about it, I was told that it was the "big annual do" of the Cariboo. It took place in October, when all the for-sale cattle were herded into our small town and bid for by buyers from many parts of the world. But it was a social time as well, starting with a colorful parade. There was plenty of excitement, pageantry, money, and liquor.

The ladies of the churches got into the act by preparing hot meals and serving them at the cattle grounds, for a price. It was their big moneymaking effort of the year, and they put everything they had into it. The man who was informing me of all this sensed a measure of hesitation in me and made it clear that I'd better go along with the whole deal because, as he said, "Your salary comes out of it."

I will never forget the woman who headed up our committee of ladies. Working like a trojan she was an organizer such as I had never seen before. She was so efficient that she had everything under control and down on paper in mid August: what kind of pie each woman would be baking, the exact hour on which day it would be picked up and by whom, and the number of the table on which the pie would be placed—for October! She was simply a genius at organization for the church. But I had never seen her in church. Sunday after Sunday I looked for her but could only conclude that she was up to her ears with the cattle sale. Once that was over and done with she'd be in church, so I thought.

No such thing! After the cattle sale when she still didn't turn up, I concluded that she was tired and must have a few weeks of rest. Anyway it wouldn't be long till Christmas, and she would surely attend during that highlight of the Christian year. I had much to learn. These events came and went. Then along about mid January I met her in the town's small post office. Convinced that this was my moment, I confronted her with the fact that although it was obvious to all how much effort she had put into the cattle sale, still I had not see her or her family in church.

Never will I forget how she stood there with arms akimbo and fire in her eyes. "Mr. Hunter," she said, "after all I do for the church, and now you ask me to come on Sundays!"

I was dumbfounded. In all my days in university and seminary, nobody ever told me how to handle a situation like that. Only days later did it dawn upon me what was wrong. Her idea of practicing Christianity was her doing all these great things *for* God. Maybe her prayer went like this, "OK, God, don't you see all I'm doing for *you*? You'd better take good care of me and my husband, because if you don't, I'll quit. And you know perfectly well there isn't another woman who could chair the cattle-sale committee and make all that money like I do."

So perhaps she thought she had God in her hands. She was dictating to him what she thought he should do and was laying it on the line. In other words, she had the gospel upside down. She was the center of her life, and God her servant.

She was trapped in what many people glibly and wearily call "church work," that burdensome thing that must be done because for some reason we think we have to support the church to keep it going. Yet it all leads to fatigue and often to cynicism. We hear it in phrases like "It's always left to the same old few" or "I've done my bit, it's time the young people took over."

Today people move frequently. Many of them, having been formerly involved in church work, make up their minds as they begin life in a new community not to become involved. "Never again," they say.

This is sad but understandable due to the false concept they have of what this ministry is. But if we were to turn the phrase around and speak of "the work of the church," new meanings would break forth. As some would say, it becomes a whole new ball game. Church work is performed out of duty. The work of the church is done from gratitude. It becomes a privilege and is therefore effortless.

This all became clear to me as I watched a woman do a simple demonstration. She had a table, a large bowl, a pitcher of water, and a small glass. "Now," she said, "the bowl represents the community, the world. The water in the pitcher is the inspiration we receive from worship. The glass is ourselves as we carry that water (inspiration) and pour it into the world." She then put a little water into the glass and poured it into the bowl. She did it several times till we got the point.

Then she did something entirely different. She held the glass over the bowl and poured until it was filled. The water soon ran over the sides. She repeated these demonstrations for quite awhile. "You see," she said, "in the first action, the glass did not have much water in it at any time, and much of the time it was entirely empty. Many Christians are like that. Half spirited they go through the motions of church work, and it is usually not very productive or satisfying. But note that in the second action the water overflowed effortlessly, the glass was always full, and the bowl got the benefit. The people represented in this illustration live on grace. They discover Christian work to be effortless and inevitable. They don't have to be coaxed or scolded or hounded into voluntary service. They look for a ministry, not church work, but the work of the church! What we do for Christ should not come from the littleness of our reserves but from the overflow of his boundless resources." So, in dramatic form she put this powerful truth. The work of the church is a privilege. It is the living out of a gift.

Witnessing is a privilege too. But here again many Christians are discouraged. They don't know how to be good witnesses. They want to influence people but constantly miss obvious opportunities.

Ralston Young is an example of a person who learned how to witness effectively and to find it a privilege. When he was a porter in New York's Grand Central Station he was ashamed of his lowly job. When people asked him what he did for a living he would say with tongue in cheek, "I'm in the leather business."

After he was converted and had given his life to Christ, he wanted to go places and do big things. When he asked God where he might best serve, God said, "Grand Central Station." So there he remained for more than thirty years, eventually calling it "my cathedral."

One day a cab drove up, and Ralston was on hand to help a woman into her wheelchair. As he began pushing her into the railway station he noticed she was weeping. Ralston prayed, "Lord, show me how I can use the very few minutes I have with this woman to witness to her." Then he looked down and said, "Ma'm, that's a mighty pretty dress you're wearing."

She looked startled and replied, "You think so? Why, I made this dress." That broke the ice.

A few minutes later he said, "Ma'm, I couldn't help but notice your crying. There must be something on your mind. Is there anything I can do to help you?"

She responded with a curt, "No!"

Now on the train, he said, "Ma'm, there must be something that is deeply troubling you. I'm a Christian, and I'll do anything to help." Still no response.

Finally he said, "Lady, would you mind if I just prayed for you?" Not being refused that, Ralston removed his cap, bowed his head, and offered up a simple prayer for her, and then made his exit.

Weeks later a young woman came running up to him

and asked if he remembered that incident. He replied that he did, vaguely. "Well," she said, "that woman in the wheelchair was my mother. Last week she died. Her final request was that I come here to search for you and to tell you that your prayer changed her life. It was the beginning of the solution to her problem. And she told me to tell you thank you."

Through countless experiences like this, Ralston Young has learned how to make use of opportunities as they come through his daily contacts with all sorts and conditions of people. He has much to give because he has greatly received. Grace, goodwill, and witness comprise the spontaneous ministry of this radiant Christian.

So life can be lived as a gift. Even problems can be accepted as gifts since every problem consists in an opportunity and a challenge waiting to be discovered. Never dull duty, worship, work, and witness become priceless privileges.

An Amazing Offer

A veteran pastor was talking to a young man who was seriously considering becoming a candidate for the ministry. In the course of conversation the pastor asked, "Would you say Christianity is essentially a demand or an offer?"

Immediately came the answer, "A demand."

The older man made no hurried reply but looked at him as if to say, "Think it through. Take some time on it. Consider it from every angle."

After a few minutes the young man spoke again, "Well, I think it is a demand and an offer, a combination of both."

Still the pastor made no direct reply. The moments dragged on as he calmly rubbed his arthritic fingers in a gesture of composure and confidence.

Then the young man spoke up. "I see what you're getting at," he said. "Christianity begins with a divine offer, and I guess that is what it is basically all the time."

He scored! From first to last, Christianity is an amazing offer. We should put this down as axiomatic: God is the great giver. He is the Great Giver because he is the Great Lover, and it is the very nature of love to want to give and give and give again. The New Testament presses home this point with the frequent use of the word *all*. Jesus said to his disciples, "*All* that I have heard from my father I have made known to you" (John

15:15 RSV). He told of the father of the prodigal who said to his elder son, "*All* that is mine is yours" (Luke 15:31 RSV). Paul writes, "He that spared not his own Son, but delivered him up for us all, how shall he not with him also freely give us *all* things?" (Rom. 8:32). Again he writes, "*All* things are yours" (I Cor. 3:21), and "having nothing, and yet possessing *all* things" (II Cor. 6:10). It would seem that this generous God, out of the infinite storehouse of his grace wants to give and give and never stop. He would lay the entire universe at our feet.

But I've heard the other view of Christianity expressed so often that I sometimes wonder if more than a very few have ever heard of grace. Many people have been drilled since childhood to regard the business of being a Christian as just contributing money and working in a local church. They have been taught this both by word and by example. Their general view of God is that he is never satisfied. He continues to make oppressive demands. He wants us to deny ourselves, to give our all, even to sacrifice. And later on, when people who have this view have tried their utmost to fulfill those demands, they find themselves constantly disappointed because they can never give enough, do enough, be faithful enough, to be inwardly satisfied. They live under the clouds of duty, obligation, yet failure. For them the good life is the restricted life, confined, with human passions suppressed. This narrow moralism dictates their every movement, their total life.

The tragedy of this misconception is that it misses the experience of Christian grace. No matter how elaborate our theology or how strict our moral code, if we miss grace, we miss everything. Without grace there is no good news but just dull religion. Without grace, goodness is not spontaneous response but dutiful obedience.

How this grace of God works can be seen in part in the experience of Bill. When I first met him I instinctively knew there was something different about this radiant man. His whole bearing, especially the way he shook hands, expressed his joy in living.

Well, he wasn't always this way. During his youth, people predicted that he would be a failure. But now he is a successful businessman. One Sunday evening he was sitting with his family in church. He proudly glanced over his wife and five children. Suddenly he was overcome with gratitude for them, for his own health, for his job, for the way everything had worked out over the past years.

And then as if from nowhere there came a voice, "Bill, I want you to work for me." He was startled. Thinking it may be the Lord speaking, he replied inwardly, "Lord, I do work for you. You know I teach in the church school and work with the youths."

Then it came again; "But I want you full time."

"I have a full-time job," Bill replied.

"Quit it. Give it up!"

What could this mean? He sat there trying to ward off this preposterous thought that had invaded him, to put down the voice and the command. But every argument he raised was met by a stronger argument from the other side. As a last resort he said, "Look at my kids. They need me."

Back came the voice, "Yes, look at my kids, the many children who have no homes, get no guidance, receive no love. They are frightened and rebellious. What about my kids?"

The thought of spending the rest of his days helping homeless kids was pretty far out. He decided to test this voice and the validity of the whole idea. So he said, "OK,

Lord, if this is you speaking, prove it to me by having that preacher up there speak my name in his sermon." Bill then drew a sigh of relief, being convinced that the matter was settled then and there.

A moment later the preacher looked straight at Bill and said, "Isn't that right, Bill?" Bill, stunned and for the moment speechless, replied, "Yes, Mr. Evans, that is right," though he didn't have a clue to what the sermon was about.

The end of the service brought the altar call. Bill went forward. After kneeling there for a while, he stood up, turned to the congregation, and blurted out quickly and quietly in very simple words, "I'm going to quit my job, and from now on I'll be helping homeless and delinquent children. Please pray for me." Then he turned around, still wondering what he had done, and tearfully faced the altar. Presently he felt a gentle hand on his shoulder. It was his wife, and she said, "Bill, I don't know what all this is about, but I'm with you all the way." And when he turned again he was looking into the faces of forty people who had come to stand with him, giving silent assurance of their support.

That marked just the beginning. At first Bill had thought he would open up a huge home where he could house several children. But all the details and red tape connected with this idea seemed insurmountable. Then one day a couple offered to take a child into their home, and then another couple wanted to do the same. By now it began to dawn on Bill that this was to be the pattern, to place children in "love homes" where families receiving the children straight from the courts could give them love, acceptance, and an atmosphere where they would experience a sense of personal respect and worth. From this the work grew; there are now sixty-seven homes giving loving care to more than a hundred fifty otherwise unwanted kids. The parents meet regularly for prayer, encouragement, and mutual help.

One rebellious boy as he was dropped off by the social worker defiantly said, "I'm only going to stay ten days." "OK," said Bill. "We'll have a real good time those ten days." When the time was up he came to Bill and said, "Papa, which comes next, fall or spring?" "Why, spring," Bill answered. "Well," the boy announced, "I'm stayin' till fall."

Bill thought, "You and me both, Johnny. We don't like to commit ourselves. We hang on, we make conditions, but, Johnny, once we let go, what a God he is!"

Bill discovered that when we respond to God's grace, that in itself turns out to be grace. Before the incident in his church, Bill's life had been surrounded by grace which was evident in his undeserved blessings and his unmerited happiness. Perhaps all this was preparation for his new and radical and costly step in ministry which launched him out on a stormy sea of new-found usefulness. In a way, we might say that his comfort and ease, when recognized as grace, led him to discomfort and a mess of problems. But he didn't resist. He knew fully what he was doing, and it was what he most deeply wanted to do. In it he continues to discover new dimensions of God's grace. What a God he is!

But, there are greater depths still. If God's grace calls forth the grace of response, as with Bill, the door is then opened to receive much more grace. Could this be the meaning of those words written by John, "Grace upon grace?" (See John 1:16 RSV.) Like a rolling snowball, grace keeps getting larger, and there is no ending. Blessings pile up, joys build up, and every response adds more possibilities.

Dorothy and Bob have five children. A few years ago they decided to adopt two children from Korea. Then they adopted two from Vietnam, both of these being paraplegics. Then there followed three from Biafra and a Siouan girl. At present they are in process of adopting a four year old from Korea.

Why do Bob and Dorothy do this? Dorothy says, "We have this opportunity to do something positive, to relieve some of the horrible frustrations we feel about war. But I get back more than I give. We were so overloaded with health, happiness, love, that I'd stand in our big kitchen and say things like, 'Holy cats, God, is all this really mine?' I don't pray by getting down on my knees and talking; so I wanted to say thanks by sharing what we had.

"I thought I was thanking God by taking in children who are crippled in some way, sharing our blessings with them. But I discovered I was being selfish as hell. When these kids started coming in, they increased what we'd been saying thank you for. Every time we'd get another, there would be more blessings. It's a circle without a middle or an end."

Dorothy has discovered that you can't outdo God's giving. Every response to grace results in more grace received. The Old Testament says, "Cast thy bread upon the waters; for thou shalt find it after many days" (Eccles. 11:1). This is generally taken to mean that charity will one day be rewarded. But the New Testament goes further, "Give, and it will be given to you; good measure, pressed down, shaken together, running over, will be put into your lap" (Luke 6:38 RSV). God responds with abundance; his grace overflows.

We could put it in a formula: grace met with gratitude

leads to more grace. When there is no gratitude, grace is stopped, cut off, hindered. Charles Kingsley wrote, "Must we not thank and thank and thank forever, and toil and toil and toil forever for him?" Yes, and in that toiling, which is response to grace, God's fresh grace flows in new depths with new blessings.

Karl Barth said, "All sin is simply ingratitude," which is a condensed version of what I've been attempting to say. Ingratitude cuts off the further grace of God. But grace, received in gratitude and recognized as grace, becomes an all-consuming experience. So Stevenson has one of his characters in *Ebb Tide* cry out: "Everything's grace. We walk upon it, we breathe it, we live and die by it, it makes the nails and axles of the universe!"

We noted that in the New Testament the word *all* is often used to refer to God's giving to us. But there is another series of *alls*. This list refers to those who respond with their all: "One thing have I desired of the Lord, . . . that I may dwell in the house of the Lord all the days of my life" (Ps. 27:4); "he goes and sells all that he has and buys that field" (Matt. 13:44 RSV); "she . . . cast in . . . all her living" (Mark 12:44).

The amazing offer of God's grace becomes more and more amazing as we respond to his all by giving our all. The process never stops.

Surprised by Grace

A man and his wife were at the local grocery store doing the family shopping. As couples do when they engage in this necessary activity, they separated so that she could pick up the regular foodstuffs, the essential things, all the while comparing prices and trying to save a penny here and a few cents there. But her husband went up and down the aisles and half-filled his basket with specialty items and tasty foods which amounted to luxury eating. He knew his wife would look over his choices and say, "We don't need this; and look at the outlandish price on that." It happened every time. She was convinced that while she saved pennies by taking time to compare and choose, he was wasting dollars on things that were nonessentials and which, therefore, shot their weekly budget into oblivion.

So they went their merry way to meet accidentally at a counter, each of them looking over the shelves of breakfast cereals and cake mixes, reading labels, and making decisions. Being only mildly aware of her he said, "Don't forget the cream."

"All right," she replied, "but don't you forget you are trying to reduce."

And then he added, "So what! You only live once."

Standing nearby was another customer who added, "But don't you think once is enough?"

"You only live once," said one man. "But don't you

think once is enough?" said the other. One wanting more life, finding days exciting and hours and seasons not long enough to crowd in everything he wants to be and do. The other expressing his true feelings, being fed up with a life composed of dreary days, being forever tired and despondent, bored with routine, and seeing no prospect of there being anything different or better.

This attitude toward life can overtake anybody. Low wages do not bring it on, nor does sickness or disappointment or tough luck. Suicides are not limited to the unemployed or to those with terminal illness. Rich people can hate this life so much that they might say, "Don't you think once is enough?" It can happen to youths whom you might think would be filled with excitement and tingling with the spirit of adventure. It can come to professional people who have a string of university degrees.

Worst of all it can happen to people who have been exposed to "religion" most of their lives, who have worked in the church and even engaged in many good works. This is the saddest situation because they are so near the good news and at the same time so far from it. Asked if they believe in God they would quickly reply, "Of course, I do." But it is likely they have never thought very much on the goodness and grace of God. To them God is some vague entity who created the world, who gave us ten commandments, and who will judge us, punish us, and consign us to hell if we don't toe the line. In the meantime he demands a lot, and we've got to keep working, giving, and serving in order to build up a good record so that when we die we can say, "See there! I haven't been so bad after all. Look what I've done! And anyway, I've been a whole lot better than my neighbor."

Such a person probably believes that although God

exists, he has his own interests, and to him people are more or less incidental. "He surely couldn't love me for myself or be interested much in me as just one insignificant person," that person might think.

Well, all this is missing the good news. I don't believe God has any interests at all except in you and me and in helping us in our discovery of the life that is exciting and full. I believe he has a thousand gifts and ten thousand blessings to give, if and when we wake up to grace.

This waking up, or we might call it being surprised by grace, this new awareness of God's abundant goodness, can happen to anybody and at the most unsuspecting times. It came to one woman as she was having her coffee after the family had gone to school and work. She said: "It was as if, in that brief moment all the love in the world was beamed on me, and I returned it with such intense joy that my eyes streamed with tears. I was cradled in the universe, loved by every living thing, time seemed non-existent, but I doubt if the experience lasted more than ten ecstatic seconds. My life has been different from that moment." Then she went on to say that in this experience she was healed, and relationships were healed. She said, "I felt profoundly loved, and I don't fear death anymore."

When the prodigal son came home he was surprised by grace. He probably expected to be punished. We might even dare to think that he hoped for justice. But as it turned out, he was surprised and overwhelmed by grace.

Grace is love that is undeserved and unexpected. You are flagged down by a police officer because you've been doing forty miles per hour in a thirty-mile zone and have been clocked by radar. After taking down all the particulars the police officer says, "Well, you were ten miles over the limit, but I'll let you off with just a warning this time." That's grace.

Or, you receive through the mail a little white envelope from a company with whom you regularly do business. You angrily tear it open muttering, "I paid them off last month. What do they want with me?" Then you read, "Dear sir, We are pleased to inform you that our records show you have been overcharged. Therefore please accept our apologies and find our check enclosed." That's like grace.

Have you ever lost something really valuable? Perhaps it was something handed down from parents and once belonged to your great-grandmother. Let's say it was gold with inlaid diamonds and was a family keepsake that became more precious each succeeding year. Suddenly it is gone. You feel sickened and guilty and ashamed. Then after several agonizing days, when you were not looking for it, it turns up. That's like grace.

Suppose that one day a parcel arrives. You open it and wonder why your friend, many miles away, should be sending anything to you. You say, "She must have gotten my birthday mixed up with someone else's. She's getting senile." Then you read the enclosed letter. "I saw this the other day when I was shopping, and it made me remember you. So I send it to you just to say I am thinking of you and am grateful for you and love you very much." No birthday or anniversary, just a pure expression of affection when there was no special occasion to call it forth. That's like grace.

Somebody thanks you for something you did a year ago that you have long since forgotten. That's grace.

One evening later, I sat with a young man who had serious problems both at work and with his family. I tried to give my best to him, but, it being the end of a very busy day, I found myself tired, eager to get this appointment over with, and be on my way home. After listening, sorting, intimating, and counseling, I suggested we pray. But it was really only half a prayer because I was longing for bed. When I said "amen," I was surprised when the young man spoke up, "And now, Mr. Hunter, may I pray for you?" He did. It was wonderful. I sat back and relaxed as he mentioned before God all the needed gifts, which gave me a new perspective, relieved my inner tension, and served to restore me from physical tiredness to fresh spirit and new energy. I was grateful for that unforgettable moment. It was grace!

Christianity is the good news of grace. If we miss this, we miss the key. One great writer says, "Grace is all we know of God and all we need to know." Let me put it this way: everybody lives his life under one of two signs—plus or minus. The prodigal, wanting the plus, discovered everything turned out to be minus. He was minus friends, minus food, minus self-respect, minus dignity, minus hope. But at home, receiving his father's grace, those minuses were turned into plusses. He was given new clothes. That was a plus he hadn't counted on. So was the banquet and all that went with it. But these were outward. There were inward plusses also: the significance of his father's kiss, his new sense of worth, his experience of new freedom. Everything changed outside, and he became a new person inside when he experienced grace.

And what a surprise! Grace and goodness and generosity were there all the time, but he didn't know it. So it is with us. Sometimes without any warning we are shocked into a recognition of the goodness of life even as we break out of the prison of the self. A man sat beside an elderly gentleman on a train. As they slowly rounded a corner he noticed a tear in the old man's eye. Then he turned and said, "Isn't it beautiful? Isn't it incredibly beautiful?" The younger man asked, "What?" He went on, "That farmer taking a load of hay up the lane and into the barn. Don't you smell it?" And he took a deep breath. "Can't you hear those wheels turning and those horses plodding? Isn't it marvelous?" The other fellow remained unmoved thinking his companion had taken leave of his senses. Then the old man explained, "You see, just awhile ago the doctor told me I have only three months to live. Ever since, everything has looked so beautiful, so important to me. You can't imagine how beautiful! I feel as if I have been asleep and only just awakened."

Psychology calls these "peak experiences during which people glimpse the essence of things, the secret of life, as if veils have been pulled aside." Experiences like these put life under the plus sign. One man said, "We get all this and heaven too."

The well-known writer Whitaker Chambers was brought to an awareness of God by holding his little daughter in his lap and being overwhelmed by the convolutions of her ears. A doctor went to a medical convention, came down for breakfast one morning, walked to a table of his friends, and said, "Have you thanked God this morning for the fluid on your eyeballs?" It has been said that Jimmy Durante, every time he came off with a successful performance, would run to the nearest phone booth, put in his dime, dial the letters *G-O-D*, say, "Thanks!" and hang up.

But all these outward plus signs, I believe, are meant to help us experience the inner life under a plus sign. New clothes, rings, and the banquet given to the prodigal were just the outer gifts to indicate that he was loved, forgiven, and embraced inside. And when grace gets on the inside of us, our perverted thinking begins to be straightened out, our complex problems become simplified, hurts are overcome, and our sick souls healed. It happens every time.

The world famous psychiatrist Dr. Paul Tournier says in his book *The Person Reborn*, "I believe that problems can be dissolved by grace like a mist that is dissipated by the sunshine." He devotes a whole chapter to the subject of grace. He goes on to say:

> People come to me for my help in solving their problems. No one knows better than I do that all human effort is powerless to solve any problem. In fact, when I try to understand their difficulties, I discover nothing but insoluble vicious circles. . . . I do not believe in their solution, but I do believe in their dissolution.

Surprised by grace! Who would have guessed that God could be that loving, and life that good? But then someone says, "Isn't this being just a little naïve? Life is made up of unfinished work, uninteresting chores, unpaid bills, unavoidable taxes, and a thousand other things that add up to making our days miserable on this earth."

Well, I suppose we can have it any way we wish. If we want to live under a minus sign, then that is our choice. But it doesn't have to be that way. When we have a wrong inner view toward life, many things go haywire. There is an old story about a man who had a piece of limburger cheese lodged in his mustache. First he blamed his food for the bad smell. Then he thought that the restaurant had a horrible odor. Then he went outside and said the world smelled rotten. Most of our grubby problems exist because we are grubby people. But we can change. We can know grace. And even though it comes as a surprise we can begin to take those first faltering steps under the plus sign, and then discover that life is good and filled with plus signs wherever we look. And all this is because we have discovered something new and exciting about God, that he is eternally good and wants to lavish his goodness on us.

The Ultimate Experience

Many reasons have been put forth for the phenomenal increase in the use of nonmedical drugs, especially by youths. Young people who know the consequences full well, who are aware of the potential damage to the brain and of the threat of possible death, nevertheless continue to indulge.

Many say they do it for "kicks." Some just want to be with the "in" crowd. Others do it out of defiance in order to assert themselves and to find freedom from convention. But one young man probably spoke for many when he said, "I take drugs because I am looking for the ultimate experience."

I am convinced we are made for ecstasy. We are never happier than when we are carried out of ourselves, than when we get ourselves lost in a drama or in something that sweeps us off our feet with beauty or awe or thrill. Some say they approach this feeling when they ski down the snowy slopes of a mountain. Others say they feel this way when listening to Beethoven's Ninth. For me it comes when I ride over the waves in a fast powerboat. Ecstasy comes when we are overwhelmed, carried away, taken momentarily out of the sordid realities of daily drudgery and routine.

But since none of these times lasts very long neither can be labeled the "ultimate experience." That can only be approximated, indicated, or simulated. If there is no ultimate experience possible, are we being mocked, teased, and finally frustrated? Does life hold out a glorious gleam before our eyes only to snatch it away so that we remain always tantalized? If this were true, then we would be forced to question the basic integrity of life itself. Where do we look for the final breakthrough?

The answer, for me at least, is in the experience of grace. This undeserved, unexpected, mostly unsought for experience of God's overwhelming generosity and love, lifting us from the gutters of self-hate, despair, and ordinary dullness and letting us know that we are loved, is a totally engulfing experience. Only those who have experienced it can testify that it is the ultimate. This is a "high" that is out of this world. It is a mind-boggler and a heart-blower. And best of all, it lasts.

Many youths who have been on drugs for months or even for years but who have discovered God's grace testify, "Man, this is beautiful." One said, "I am stoned. I'm stoned on Jesus. Only it's far better than being stoned on drugs. Drugs are down. This is the most incredible 'up' in the world. I feel like I'm floating all the time, with Jesus." Another says, "It's so neat! It's out of sight! It's a gas! It frees you from fear! It's superedifying!" So all at once these youths feel they have what they've searched and sought and hungered for but in self-destroying ways.

Grace. What is it? How do you describe it? Grace is not something you can easily explain. I can't say I know fully what it is. (Does anybody?) Nevertheless, I can recognize it when I see it or feel it in myself.

Anna and I were in Sweden. We set out eagerly one morning with a group of people to scale a mountainside. We were particularly excited because the territory was very familiar to the late Dag Hammarskjöld. As a youth he would hike on these trails, camp overnight along the way, and meditate from the heights.

Going up was much easier than I had expected. I was amazed that I wasn't tired or impatient with the slow progress we made during the several hours of our ascent. After reaching a point high enough to give us a magnificent view of the distant mountains of Norway, we began our descent. Going down turned out to be the most difficult, dangerous, and exhausting aspect of the entire venture. A gentle rain had begun falling, and the path was slippery. We slid and fell and picked our way over rocks. Then it turned cold; there was no more distant view, and our feet began to ache. It was slow going. From time to time we stopped to rest. A couple of jokers in the crowd tried to humor us with funny stories, but we weren't much in the mood for laughing. The trail seemed never to end, and we were soaked through.

Then we heard some happy voices, saw smoke curling amidst the low fir trees, and caught a glimpse of a little fire made in a depression of rock. People from the valley, thinking about us and our possible needs, had come up the trail to meet us. They brought hot buns and fresh coffee they had made. Never did food taste so good! In moments we had joined the crowd, eating, drinking, singing, and warming ourselves. What remains with me after this incident is that we had done nothing but receive. The goodness of those buns and that hot drink will linger in my memory. It did more than satisfy our hunger. It warmed our hearts. We had tasted grace.

I couldn't help but think of the time when Jesus, after his resurrection, called to his disciples from the shore. They had been up all night fishing. They were wet and hungry and cold and tired and discouraged. He called,

"Come and have breakfast." Feeling their human needs
he had a fire going and fish frying. He hadn't come to
blame them for deserting him before his death. He had
come to reaffirm his love for them. Fire and food and
forgiveness and fellowship were all theirs at once, typical
of God's magnificent magnanimity. (See John 21:12
RSV.)

Because grace is the ultimate experience, it cannot be
fully expressed or reported in words. Language fails at
this point. Peter simply says, "You are transported with
a joy too great for words" (I Peter 1:8 NEB); and Paul
reflects the same, "Thanks be to God for his inexpres-
sible gift" (II Cor. 9:15 RSV).

When we truly experience this grace we discover we
cannot hold back the gratitude. This is the most
cleansing and motivating power we can ever know.
Envy, jealousy, resentment, and similar dark and sinister
attitudes can't exist alongside such gratitude.

Our son John was away at college. At Easter break,
while many of his friends traveled far for winter sports or
southern sunshine, he simply came home. I thought that
he might be feeling envious of those who were on a
glamorous holiday. But my anxiety vanished when he
wrote to us after his return to classes, "All the kids who
went down South for the break came back with lovely,
bright tans. I came back with a tan inside, and for that I
am thankful." He had felt a touch of grace, and that was
good. But more: his letter was grace to us, his parents.
No expensive holiday anywhere in the world could have
provided anything better than that for either of us.

This is part of the "hidden wisdom" Paul talks about.
It is a strong impetus to Christian goodness, generosity,
and good works of every kind. These are qualities of life
our world needs at the present time and many people

deeply desire, but they cannot be created or demanded or legislated. No censorship of morality will instill in people a desire for honest love, just dealings, open relationships. But grace inspires gratitude, and gratitude inspires obedience and service. As one man put it, "When the thing you ought to do becomes the thing you want to do, you're free."

Paul spoke of the "grace of generosity which God has imparted" (II Cor. 8:1 NEB). To the Ephesians, he writes about "the richness of God's free grace lavished upon us" (Eph. 1:8 NEB). Without this experience the resources of our own generosity will dry up, especially since we live in a time of rising costs, increased taxes, and the shrinking dollar.

Many otherwise big-hearted people wonder how they can afford to be generous. The basic costs of living seem to use up just about their entire income. A clue to the answer can be seen in the case of a friend of mine who, when his church launched a stewardship campaign, pledged far more than was expected of him. Asked to explain his generosity he simply stated, "Well, I've discovered something. When I shovel out, the Lord shovels in, and he's got a much bigger shovel than I have." This man had experienced the blessing that comes from generosity. For although God himself is the original generous giver, our response in kind only enables him to be more generous—and in surprisingly new ways.

I know an astute businessman who carries this spirit of generosity into his office and even to his bill-paying. On his company check forms he has printed, "It is a privilege to pay." Some people may think this is carrying things a little far, but if you knew this man and how exuberant and enthusiastic he is about life and all God's gifts, you would understand why he feels this way.

So goodness, generosity, and all kinds of good works spring out of the grateful heart that responds to the experience of grace. This is just the opposite of dutiful service, Spartan obedience, or rigid rule-following. There is an ancient story of an event that took place in the slave market of Cairo. It seems that one day a very wealthy man put up a high bid on a slave. He paid his price and later handed the slave a piece of paper on which was written, "This is your emancipation. I love to set men free."

The slave stood in utter bewilderment. He couldn't believe it. Was he dreaming? Then turning to the man he asked, "Do you mean I am free to go anywhere I choose and do anything I like?"

"Yes," came the answer.

"Then," he said, "what I really want to do most is to serve you the rest of my days."

So now, while his daily routine probably remained about the same, he was working under an entirely new kind of relationship, being newly motivated to willing service.

Something like that has taken place between God's first revealing himself through law and his full self-giving through grace. This is why the new covenant supplants the old. John says, "The law was given by Moses, but grace and truth came by Jesus Christ" (John 1:17). Paul put it to the Roman Christians, "We are discharged from the law, to serve God in a new way" (Rom. 7:6 NEB).

Perhaps there is no better illustration of grace than the experience of the Prodigal when he returned home.

When he started his weary and sad steps toward his father's house he was a broken man, penniless, friendless, useless. But what surprise awaited him! How the father's heart burst open with lavish love and amazing grace! The boy probably never knew such grace existed—let alone for him.

Someone has said that if the father had just allowed him back on the property, that would have been mercy. To have talked over a plan whereby the young man could have made amends for his foolish waste of resources, that would have been justice. To have met him at the front door and offered him a sandwich and coffee, that would have been forgiveness. To have given the boy just what he asked for, namely, to be made a servant along with the many others who worked for his father, would have been more than fair. But to run a long distance to meet him, to greet him with kisses, to provide a banquet and music and invited guests; to cover him with princely robes; and present him with jewelry, well, this goes beyond all expectations. It is an act of grace! Because of it the Prodigal Son had the ultimate experience.

Nothing less than this will finally satisfy any of us. All else is substitute, and if someone is tempted to criticize the father for losing his head and showing too much generosity, let him imagine the joy and gratitude in the father's heart that could not be contained. Listen to him as he goes to the elder brother who is sulking in his jealousy and tries to explain, "We had to celebrate and show our joy" (Luke 15:32 Phillips). In other words, "We had no choice. It was impossible for us to contain our happiness."

Life has nothing more ecstatically wonderful than that, nor can we imagine anything greater. And it isn't just a momentary flash, a once-in-a-lifetime spree. When once we begin to feel the flow of God's grace within us, it becomes a permanent part of our daily life and total outlook. It affects everything we think and do. Grace is life's ultimate experience.

Cutting the Cake

The church was appropriately decorated for the big event. Enthusiastic people crowded the pews, and I had been invited to bring the message to the one hundredth anniversary. Right from the start I could sense something different about this occasion, not the least being the three-tiered cake sitting in all its delicious splendor on the table immediately below the pulpit and in full view of everybody. Following my remarks, the minister stood to say something I had never heard in a worship service before, "We will now worship God by cutting the cake."

The scene and those words stuck with me. As I thought about it I became more and more excited about the idea of Christian living being like cutting the cake. Once we come under the experience of grace, "cutting the cake" becomes the name of the game.

Jesus told about a king who gave a great banquet in honor of his son and new daughter-in-law. (See Matt. 22:1–14.) It was a lavish feast and several VIPs were there. But many who were invited refused to come. They all had their own reasons I suppose, according to their schedules and personal priorities. So, since there was still plenty of room, the king sent his servants into the streets to invite anybody and everybody. And did they come! Every seat was filled, and a good time was had by all.

One fellow was so much in a hurry to get in on the festivities that he didn't take time to go home, clean up, and put on a fresh shirt. He came just as he was—dungarees, sweater, and beat-up shoes—and there he stood in sharp contrast to the other guests wearing fine clothes. When the king caught sight of him he was angry and felt the man was taking advantage of the situation. He was an embarrassment to the king; so he had him thrown out.

What is the point of this story? Is real life—life in the kingdom of God and of grace—like a feast? Yes! And the feast means everything that goes along with the sumptuous food: music and dancing and fun and laughter and good conversation.

The point is, the banquet is prepared for us and we are invited. Just to be asked, is grace. We cannot come because of our desire to but only in response to the invitation. This is good news to a world starving for basic life-satisfactions, where many have never heard that they are invited or even that there is a banquet.

The picture of feasting is a recurring one in scripture. Isaiah said, "Come, buy wine and milk without money and without price. . . . Eat, . . . and let your soul delight itself in fatness" (Isa. 55:1, 2). In the Twenty-third Psalm, the height of grace is reached in the words "Thou preparest a table before me in the presence of my enemies" (v. 5 RSV). Jesus told of the ten virgins who were invited to the marriage supper. When the prodigal came home he was given a dinner party.

But how does God communicate to us the fact that there is a banquet? Well, one way is through the goodness of the world itself, a fact that we often take for granted. A man who had been blind for a long, long time had a cornea-transplant operation, and after many years he was able to see. "Everything looked beautiful," he said. "I saw white and black and color and symmetry. There was the beauty of people. Children played in the driveway. An old lady walked toward us and passed. I felt no great thrill that I was no longer blind; only the awful sense of beauty thrilled me to the limit of my endurance. I hurried into the house and to my room and buried my head in the pillow. I had not the capacity to digest so much grandeur. I wept."

But even more than the world around us, God communicates the feast idea through people. Much of the time we may think of people as just objects in our way. But every once in a while the glory and wonder and mystery of people confront us. For instance, in one scene of Thornton Wilder's play *Our Town*, Emily, who had died at the age of twenty-six, is given the opportunity of returning to earth to relive one day of her life, whatever day she chooses. She can relive it but she cannot change it. So she chooses to come back on the day of her twelfth birthday. Now, with her perspective of eternity and her infinitely heightened sensitivity, she is affected deeply by even the simplest events of that day. Her father comes in from work and is exhausted. Her mother is fussing about the kitchen getting the meal ready and baking the cake. In the midst of it Emily pleads: "Mama, just look at me one minute as though you really saw me. . . . Mama! Fourteen years have gone by, I'm dead. . . . But just for a moment now we're all together. Mama, just for a moment we're happy. Let's look at one another."

Of course no one hears her, for she is just experiencing her already-lived day. She can stand it no longer and cries out: "I can't. I can't go on. It goes too fast. We don't have time enough to look at one another. . . . I didn't realize . . . all that was going on, and we never noticed.

. . . O earth, you're too wonderful for anybody to realize you."

Then, she turns to the stage manager and asks through her tears, "Do any human beings ever realize life while they live it . . . every, every minute?"

What a banquet! Seeing it from Emily's perspective, life's daily happenings, common conversations, ordinary activities, become a feast of good things.

When the prodigal came home he found more than just a feast of food. Love and acceptance and forgiveness and inner peace and self-worth and hope and a hundred other things were laid on the table before him. People who have experienced this surge of good things within them are lost for words to describe it. One man said, "I felt I was in love with everybody. I could have put my arms around the whole world." A woman said, "I felt engulfed by love." Another, "For the first time in my life I felt really clean." Still another: "The ecstasy lasted only for a few moments, but the glow will go on forever. I discovered there is hope for this messed-up life of mine."

E. Stanley Jones said, "Christians have more joy per square inch than anybody else has to the square mile." Bishop Gerald Kennedy put it this way, "The Christian has more excitement in a minute than the men of the world have in a year."

The invitation to the banquet is rebuffed by two types of people: those who are oblivious to it and those who make excuses. It is true that many never hear about any banquet at all. Life to them is grim and demanding. They are forever trying to make the grade. They seldom, if ever, lift up their eyes because they do not believe there is anything worth seeing.

I was sitting with a friend on his lanai, overlooking Waikiki and the blue Pacific. Expressing my admiration for the view, I was told of an incident of the day before. It had been raining most of the morning. At about noon he saw a magnificent rainbow that stretched from the low land on the one side to the water on the other. As my friend and his wife stood enthralled by it, they noticed a sailboat coming along not too far from shore that moved right into the rainbow. "Isn't it marvelous," he said to his wife, "to think that the people in that boat are engulfed in so much splendor?" She agreed but went on to say, "Isn't it too bad that they have no awareness of it all?"

Of course she was right. Rainbows can be seen only at a distance, never when you're in the midst of one. This is the case with God's banquet for those who will not look. Life, to them, is stern necessity, and they won't be convinced otherwise.

But many who do see, refuse the invitation just the same.

Their excuses are usually pretty thin: they have other things to do; they don't like meeting people; they really want to come, but later; now isn't convenient. They don't want to be involved; there must be a mistake; they can't believe the invitation was for them, somebody got the names mixed up. Meanwhile life goes on in its boredom, frustration, dissatisfaction, dullness, and despair, the only relief being an invitation of a different kind, "Let's get drunk."

To be sure, much of this is caused by a wrong view of God. God the judge, God the celestial policeofficer, is the prevalent idea of many who never see the inside of God's banquet hall. A man said, "As a kid, I was brought up to think of God as a big man with a club who went around looking for boys who were having fun so that he could put a stop to it."

But in spite of all, some come. Who? The nobodies! In the story it is the poor, the crippled, the blind, and the lame. Add the beggars, prostitutes, swindlers, broken-down wretches of humanity, people who stand in lineups waiting for a handout or a job interview. Add the host of faithful people who sit at desks all day or who wait on tables or who serve customers from behind counters. Add repair persons, carriers, maintenance workers, and all who plod on through the years with little or no change in their work and who feel like a small cog in a vast machine. Yet, the amazing thing is that out of a number of ordinary people, some do hear the invitation and decide to respond.

For those who come, the persistent questions are: Why me? What did I do to deserve this? Does God want me with my vile disposition, my ineptitude, my bungling, my lazy habits, or with my talentless self? The idea seems too good to be true. Paul never could discover a satisfactory answer to why God had been so generous with him. "I am less than the least of all God's people; yet God gave me this privilege of taking to the Gentiles the Good News about the infinite riches of Christ" (Eph. 3:8 TEV).

But it is just this amazement and God's goodness and our total unworthiness that make us acceptable at the banquet. This is our proper clothing. The man who came in without being clothed in humility, wonder, and gratitude was declared unacceptable and was thrown out. He came but on his own terms. God's grace is available to all, but we cannot presume upon it, or it doesn't come as grace.

My favorite comic strip is "Peanuts." I suppose the reason so many find it intriguing is that in a sense we are all kids at heart. We identify with the little characters, and we can see in their antics how much of our serious daily living is just game-playing. Their simple but pointed remarks puncture our pomposity. And maybe if we could see our problems reduced to a baseball diamond, we would have a better perspective on much that causes us worry and concern.

Recently there was a strip in which Lucy writes a letter to Santa Claus: "Dear Santa, do you need a secretary to help during the holiday season? I could answer letters and run errands, and I will work for only five hundred dollars a week."

Charlie Brown jumps to exclaim, "Five hundred dollars a week!" Lucy says, "Why not? Everybody knows the old guy is loaded!"

A man said, "God will forgive; that's his business." Such an attitude makes one shudder. It says that God's grace is being taken advantage of. It is being exploited. Just as the man in Jesus' parable was prevented from participating in the banquet, so taking grace for granted cuts us off from the good things God has in mind to give.

Something happens between accepting the invitation and entering the banquet hall. Awed at being invited, we instinctively want to be changed. We are open to the birth of a new spirit, a new attitude, and a new desire. So God's goodness has done its work in us. He wins us not by scolding and condemning but by smothering us in kindness, deluging us with goodness, and lavishing us with grace. He wears down our resistance and brings us to repentance by a love that continues in spite of our reluctance. In fact, if only God were not so good, we might feel we could hold him off or run from him as a boy runs from a bad-tempered father. But it doesn't happen that way. God is good and we can't change that! And now something inside us makes us want to change to be worthy of that goodness. We never can be, but we still want to try.

Victor Hugo expresses this idea perfectly in his classic story of Jean Valjean. He was the man who broke into the apartment of the bishop and stole a pair of golden candlesticks. Caught red-handed by the police, the culprit was soon returned to the scene of the crime and thrown down in front of the bishop, who, seeing the pathos in his eyes, turned to the police and calmly said, "Why, I gave him those candlesticks." The authorities were bewildered but could do nothing else than let the man off. After they were gone, the bishop put his arm around the thief and said, "Jean my brother, you belong to God now."

So God uses people to communicate goodness. I have a friend who is as enthusiastic about people as he is exuberant about life. I had not seen him for a long time, and our latest communication was not marked by complete openness. I had criticized him and then ignored him. One day I heard he was speaking in a certain place; so I decided to hear him. Afterward, with some hesitation I walked up to exchange greetings. I would have preferred to go straight home, but thinking he might have seen me in the audience I didn't feel I could leave without at least offering a hello. So I was quite prepared for a handshake and "How are you?" But to my amazement and surprise he literally took me in his big arms, expressed his thorough delight at seeing me again, and with gestures of magnanimity let me know that the past was gone, and we were brothers in Christ. The experience of that undeserved goodness humbled my heart, and every time I recall it, it pulls me to God's love.

It's a feast, a banquet, a smorgasbord of goodness that God offers. He says, "I want you to come. It's all for you. And I want you to help cut the cake."

We may have been putting him off for years, but we can still come. And that's worth knowing. It's great good news.

Health Is Yours—Take It!

This heading may seem harsh and insensitive, especially to people who are desperately trying to find health but have been battling chronic illness for years. And there are many who would fit into this category. Perpetually unwell, they may continually turn to drugs, which too often become a dependency, and be forever on the lookout for some new chemical that promises vigor and vitality.

Yet statements from many experts, the perspective of the Bible, and my own experience all witness to the conviction that health is one of God's gifts, if and when we are ready to receive. If "all things are yours" as Paul said (I Cor. 3:21 RSV), surely health is on the list somewhere, probably near the top because it is so important to every person.

The other day a woman died in one of our city hospitals, the victim of malnutrition. Eighty-one years old, she had literally starved to death; yet it was discovered later that she had all kinds of money in her apartment and over fifty thousand dollars in bank accounts. It is difficult to have much sympathy for such a person who has abundant resources but doesn't make use of them.

But isn't that just what so many of us do in regard to health? We want healing or bodily wholeness; yet by our actions, attitudes, habits, or indulgences we become the enemy of ourselves and our own deepest desires. While God wants to give us life that is full and abundant, exciting and whole, and while we desire to be well and strong with plenty of energy and vitality, we so often struggle under the burdens of half health. The question is, How can we take this gift and appropriate it for ourselves?

Well, one way of taking it is to have what I call a "control center" in our lives. I have a policeman friend, who educated me on a fact of our life in the busy city. He told me that in downtown Toronto there is a computer that controls every traffic signal in our metropolitan area populated by more than 2 million people. I had thought that every light was on its own, but because so many turn red just as I get to them, it seems that the lights have some special hostility against me.

But, no, one light works in conjunction with another under orders from the central computer to facilitate the flow of traffic, particularly during peak hours.

We need a similar control center in our lives. We are very complex beings with a body that is a fantastically intricate mechanism, a mind that not only remembers but thinks, creates new ideas, and imagines unbelievable possibilities, to say nothing about deep feelings and emotions, as well as our spiritual dimension which reflects the very nature of God. Not to have a control center for all this is to live in the midst of a confusing jumble of forces, most of the time working against one another.

When we have given ourselves over to Christ, he becomes the control center of our lives. He gives us his Spirit, and Paul says, "To be controlled by the Spirit results in life and peace" (Rom. 8:6 TEV). So when illness comes, such as indigestion, insomnia, colds, headaches, and the like, we have to ask ourselves in all honesty, Who or what has been controlling us? If it is because of undisciplined eating or tiredness that we have allowed our sleep to be robbed by anxious thought or by some burning resentment, or our minds controlled by bitterness and an unforgiving attitude, then we have clearly blocked the health-giving processes.

E. Stanley Jones tells what happened in him that allowed him to discover new health. He was a young man, not yet having completed his first term in India. The pressures of his work had brought on exhaustion and a nervous breakdown. After repeated attempts to overcome which led only to failure and more discouragement, it was decided he should go back to America and take a year to recover. Having done that and now returned to India, the old trouble came again. It looked as if his whole career would be stopped, and his life's calling questioned.

One night he was in the back of a church in Lucknow when he heard a voice asking, "Are you ready for the work to which I have called you?" He answered, "No, Lord, for I am done for. I'm at the end of my rope." The voice continued, "Well, if you will turn that over to me, I will look after it." Stanley Jones answered, "Lord, I close the bargain right there."

Reporting this years later, he said,

A great peace settled in my heart and pervaded me. I knew it was done. Life, abundant life, had taken possession of me. For weeks after that I hardly knew I had a body. I worked long days and often far into the night, and I would come down to bedtime wondering why on earth I should ever go to bed at all. There wasn't a trace of tiredness of any kind. Nine of the most strenuous years of my life have gone since then, and I have never known such health. It was more than just a physical touch. I had tapped new resources for body, mind, and spirit. And *I had done nothing but take it.—The Christ of the Indian Road,* McClelland and Stewart, Toronto, 1926, p. 20.

So with a new control center he could take the health that was available to him.

A second step in taking this gift of health is to bring every aspect of our lives into harmony with what we know to be God's will and purpose. Paul talks about living "in union with Christ Jesus" (Rom 8:1 TEV). The healthy person is the harmonious person. One of the world's most renowned physicians is Dr. Paul Tournier. He writes in *The Meaning of Persons:*

> Most illnesses do not come as a bolt from the blue. The ground has probably been prepared for years. Faulty diet, intemperance, overwork or moral conflicts have been slowly eroding our vitality. One medical doctor said, most people don't die, they kill themselves. Every act of physical, psychological or moral disobedience of God's purpose is an act of wrong living and has inevitable consequences.

So we might say that to the degree we live harmoniously with the Infinite Spirit of life and are open to the divine inflow, we help in setting into operation those forces that will eventually result in abounding health and strength.

The medical profession is now telling us that practically all disease with all the suffering involved has its origin in perverted mental and emotional states and conditions. Dr. Hans Selye, Canada's foremost research scientist, puts it down to stress. Stress is the cause of all disease, he says. Sidney Jourard, professor of psychology, University of Florida, says that he imagines a family of germs looking for a home where they can multiply and flourish. He says that if he were the leader of that family of germs, he would avoid like the plague anyone who is productively and enjoyably engaged in living and loving. He would wait until the person had lost hope, became discouraged, felt ground down by the requirements of respectable role-playing. Then, at that precise moment, he would invade! "The body is as fertile then as a well manured flower bed is for the geranium" *(The Transparent Self)*.

So inner harmony, peace of mind, a positive outlook, are vitally important to health. A Johns Hopkins doctor says, "We do not know why it is that worriers die sooner than nonworriers, but that is a fact." Disharmony invites disease. It has been suggested that no disease can enter or take hold of us unless it finds something in us that corresponds to itself. The same is true with ideas and attitudes. For instance, when someone comes to the door of our house and rings the bell, whoever answers has the decision as to whether this person will come in or stay out. For instance, at the present time my wife is trying to make do with a vacuum cleaner that has long since passed its best days. It no longer rolls from one room to another but has to be picked up with both hands and lovingly carried. Otherwise it will fall into many pieces. I'm not sure which will last longer, my wife's patience or this dilapidated machine. The point is, if someone came to our door selling vacuum cleaners, he would probably have no trouble getting inside to make his pitch. His desire would meet our need.

In the same way, when diseases come to us and seek entrance, our inner needs and wants and attitudes determine whether they invade us or are turned away. If we say to ourselves "I think I'm catching a cold," and then begin to think fearful thoughts about having to suffer through the next number of days with all the attending miseries, it is probable that those fears will lower the resistive forces within. Our very thought processes help destroy the protective and life-building energy of the body; and so the germs are admitted, even invited. When a person says, "I'm sick with worry," this is probably an exact description of what is happening. It was said of a certain man, "He died of grudgitis."

Some time ago I suffered from a severe cold that extended into more of me and was more weakening than any I could remember. Moreover, it came just at a peak period of activity when I needed to be at my best. But there I lay, helpless because of a few measly little germs. I was resentful and disappointed and embarrassed all at the same time.

Then I began to analyze my own habits of the previous week or so. I had had several late-night and early-morning engagements. I'd thrown caution to the wind and eaten rich desserts and sometimes a double portion. A "friend" had given us a large box of chocolates, and I'd let my hand get into them many times in the day. There were a few people with whom I was on bad terms, and I kept reviewing our festering relationship as I lay sleeplessly in bed. When I couldn't sleep because of my desire to get back at them, I came downstairs and had something more to eat on the theory that it would help the blood go from my head to my stomach and thus let me rest. Then it only took a minor fracas with my wife, two or three little scrapes with my family, and I was a goner! I became fully receptive to anything that happened to come along, and those cold germs soon invaded and took over.

The personal inventory was good because it not only allowed me to see the process but challenged me not to take the next wrong step of self-pity. In all honesty I had to admit that all this had come by my own deliberate choices.

So whether it is medical insights, biblical teachings, or my own experiences, all corroborate the fact that life works best when Christ is in control and when we bring all aspects of life into harmony with his will and purpose. Paul says, "The body . . . is for the Lord—and the Lord for the body" (I Cor. 6:13 NEB).

Take Today

My wife and I were guests at a twenty-fifth anniversary; it was a gala occasion. More than two hundred people attended, some coming many miles to be a part of the celebration. The man and wife whom we were honoring were bedecked in fine clothes. She sported a beautiful orchid. There were gifts and fine speeches, congratulations, introductions of special people, all followed by a delicious luncheon and a huge cake, so large that everybody had a generous helping. Yes, it was a memorable evening.

The celebration wasn't for their marriage. It marked twenty-five years of sobriety! The event was sponsored by Alcoholics Anonymous, and the special guests were Byrnes and Mary Fleuty, two of God finest witnesses, and very special people to a vast number of struggling and growing Christians.

It all began one evening in November, 1950. Previously there had been years of growing addiction to alcohol, which led finally to compulsive drinking. Mary had been ill, and in her recuperation a physician had suggested that she would be helped by taking a little sherry. She was shocked because she had been raised in a home where alcohol in any form was not tolerated. But, following doctor's orders, she obtained the bottle. To her surprise and delight she discovered she liked it. And so began a steady trek toward alcoholism. It overtook both of them even to the point that they could no longer carry on their daily work. Their drinking was in the daytime, in the evening, anytime, all the time and continued for many years.

Then came that eventful night when they were at a party in a local hotel. Just as they were getting into the serious drinking of the evening a strange thing happened. Mary was about to lift a glass to her lips when she heard a voice say, "Put that down, you've had your last drink." She looked around to see who it might have been. Nobody was close. She proceeded to lift the glass again. Again it came clearly and decisively, "Put that down, you've had your *last* drink."

Calling Byrnes she said, "I want to go home."

"But the evening's just getting started," he replied.

"Never mind, I want to go home," Mary insisted.

Byrnes consented, and on the way home she shared with him her startling experience. Together they talked and began to look at themselves, and for the first time they took an honest inventory of where they were and in what direction they were going. After several hours, Mary announced that she, as of that night, was through with drinking. Byrnes replied, "Well, if you've had your last, then I've had my last drink too."

In the next few days they sought out their local minister who said that the voice was probably God's speaking to Mary. Mary felt deeply convicted of the fact that God was wanting into her life, wanted to claim her and change her. From that, they began to attend church, join groups, read the Bible, and attend the local Alcoholics Anonymous sessions.

And how they have been used through this quarter century! Their home has been a center of counseling and loving acceptance for hundreds upon hundreds of people. They have had groups serving many needs and have developed counseling skills in helping people that produce amazing results in seemingly the most hopeless situations. No one knows how many middle-of-the-night calls they have received from persons who have perhaps been thrown out of some inner-city tavern and have no place to go. Mary and Byrnes will leave their bed, get dressed, and drive miles looking for the forsaken soul, and then bring that person home to spend the night. Often those one-nights have extended to weeks or months.

The personal cost of their ministry is not known, recorded, or even mentioned. Their time and energy are at the disposal of human need in whatever form it presents itself. They have dried out drunks, fed them, nursed them back to stabilization; found jobs; counseled; prayed; and agonized with them, and sometimes been hated for it all in the end.

One morning I was having coffee in their kitchen when a prominent lawyer whose life had been destroyed almost by his drinking and who had been their "house guest" now for several weeks, stalked out. Before slamming the door, he yelled back, "I never want to see you again." A few moments later we could hear his tires squeal as he spun them onto the pavement in a dramatic takeoff. Mary, looking down simply and calmly, said, "He'll be back." Sure enough, within one week there came the familiar voice over the phone, "I'm sorry. I didn't know what I was doing. Please let me come back." So Mary and Byrnes Fleuty have learned the tricks, heard the stock-in-trade arguments, and come to know well the evasive techniques of the alcoholic personality.

And now their twenty-fifth anniversary of sobriety! The guest speaker, also an alcoholic and a professor at the university, said, "No matter how long an alcoholic has been sober, he is only one drink away from being a drunk."

Mary said, "Yes, it has been 25 years, 9,125 days!" I perked up my ears. How come she knew the number of days? The A.A. program calls for living one day at a time. The member soon learns that he must never say "I've quit drinking" or "I'm now free from alcohol." The very best he can ever say is, "I didn't have a drink today." Cockiness often leads to a fall. One person said, "If you've been sober for 24 hours, the program is working for you."

Well, as I sat and listened and pondered the significance of the evening, there came to mind some words in the 118th Psalm: "This is the day which the Lord has made; let us rejoice and be glad in it" (v. 24 RSV). If the alcoholic must learn to live one day at a time, it is a truth for all of us to follow.

Then I remembered a weekend conference that I had attended a few years ago. Coming down in the morning I found I was one of five around the breakfast table. Some of us were only partly awake because it was an early hour. We were joined by a chipper fellow who greeted us, "Good morning, everybody, this is the day." A bit startled we wondered what he knew that we didn't. After a few moments one man walked into the trap by asking, "What day?" Our new friend was waiting for that and shot back, "The day the Lord has made."

It was a good reminder. For the Christian, no day is just another day or simply the day after the night before. It is always *the* day. No two days are alike. Each day has its own peculiar opportunities and possibilities. Listen to this old poem from the Sanskrit called "The Salutation of the Dawn":

Take Today

Look to this Day, for it is life—
The very Life of Life!
In its brief course lie all the Verities
And Realities of your Existence:
The Bliss of Growth,
The Glory of Action, The Splendor of Beauty;
For Yesterday is but a Dream,
And To-morrow is only a Vision;
But To-day, well lived
Makes every Yesterday a Dream of Happiness,
And every To-morrow a Vision of Hope.
Look well, therefore, to this day!

A modern writer put it thus:

There is in each new day the witchery of the unexpected. It inflames my curiosity. It appeals to my sense of the undiscovered. It is a packet of surprises. It comes, grey and unpretentious, but it invariably brings its own thrills and sensations and astonishments. It is a slice of infinity. It tingles with the unexpected. And so it will be to the last.

A minister friend was a guest in a home over a weekend. When he lifted his blind in the morning he saw something written on the glass. It turned out to be Psalm 118:24. When he asked about it at breakfast, his hostess said, "Well, you see, I used to be a terrible worrier. I was always afraid of what would happen tomorrow, and each morning when I woke up I felt as though I had the weight of the world upon me. Then one morning when I was very upset about things, I sat down and read my Bible. I came across these words, 'This is the day.' Then I noticed that this didn't pertain to any special day but to every day. And why should I be afraid of the days if God makes them? It flashed upon my mind like a burst of sunshine on a gloomy day. So I had a man with a diamond scratch the words upon the glass. Now I see those words every morning. Somehow you don't feel afraid of the day if you feel that God made it."

We are told by some psychologists that the first five minutes in any day are decisive. In this time slot, attitudes are formed and moods established. And to say "I will rejoice and be glad in it" is to affirm the day, to embrace it, and to accept it as God's unique gift. Once that is done, the question of how the day is to be used comes naturally and is practically unavoidable.

I have discovered that when I follow this acceptance and affirmation of the day, I have a new appreciation of the uniqueness of my total situation and its special quality. One time I found myself saying, "This is the house the Lord has given me, I'll rejoice and be glad in it." That ruled out some complaints I had about my house as well as all envy or covetousness of other people's houses.

"This is the job the Lord has given me, I'll rejoice and be glad in it." Everybody finds some aspects of his or her job both exhausting and perhaps boring. But all of a sudden I saw new possibilities in my job as I affirmed it and accepted it as God's gift.

"This is the family the Lord has given to me." How often I have wished that certain members of my family would be different or better than they are! But now I could see each of them in his or her special individuality and love each despite idiosyncrasies. What had been a trial to my patience now became the source of personal pride and appreciation.

"This is the body the Lord has made." Many people have never accepted or affirmed their bodies. They are too tall or too short or too something. The day I accepted my body as God's unique and special gift was a day of discovery of a new freedom that I never dreamed possible.

At the twenty-fifth-anniversary celebration mentioned

above, a woman gave a brief account of her pilgrimage from alcoholism. She told us how her thinking was so terribly mixed up. She said, "The alcoholic is a tense cat. Negative thinking is cunning, baffling, and powerful. But the change came in my life when I learned to begin each day with this prayer, 'Lord, direct my thinking.'"

I was called to visit a woman in hospital. Her husband told me that the doctors could find no physical reason for her defeatist attitudes. She had always been a cheerful, bubbly, fun-loving person, full of good humor, but for the past several months she had been in depression. In fact, her outlook was so negative she kept saying she didn't want to live anymore. She took no interest in her family. Her friends meant nothing. She had no desire to do anything. When she took the prescribed drugs she only felt more useless still. Her husband suggested their going on a trip to some new and exciting part of the world, but she replied that she didn't want to go anywhere. He told me that the only thing she really wanted to do was sleep and added, "She can't even do that restfully."

I visited her both in the hospital and at home. Then, after many hours of listening to her situation, I suddenly remembered that when I was a pastor in a former church we had "Text of the Month." The first Sunday of each month we would distribute to everybody a little printed inspirational text. It was on sticky paper, and we urged that it be placed where a person might see it many times in a day, memorize it, and then apply it. So I suggested to this woman that she get a piece of paper and write on it a verse from the Bible, "I can do all things in him who strengthens me" (Phil. 4:13 RSV).

She asked, "What good will it do?"

"I don't know but let's try it," I replied.

Feeling that she wasn't very enthusiastic about the idea I asked her, "Do you really want to get out of this depression?"

"Yes, I really do. I've had about all of it I can take," she answered.

"Do you really want to function normally, to be off all these medications, and to be your happy self?"

"Yes, I want that more than anything else," she replied.

Reluctantly she consented to my suggestion. Then I proposed that she place the scripture in some prominent place where she couldn't miss seeing it many times during the day.

In ten days, what a difference! She greeted me with a smile, the first I'd ever seen on her face. She said, "It's working. I put that paper on my bedroom mirror; so I see it first thing every morning. Then I wrote out another one and put it on the medicine cabinet, then another for the kitchen windowsill, and still another for the dashboard of the car." It was obvious she was a new person but still in the process of even greater change. Within a month she was well and taking her part in home, church, and community. Her life now was an affirmation of health, and her countenance radiated her joy in living. She learned how to take hold of each day.

There is a story about two turtles. The younger one was complaining that things moved too slowly for him. The rabbit would bound past, the birds soared, but the best he could do was inch along. The old turtle listened for a while and then said, "Listen to me, you young gaffer, if there's anything a young turtle has to learn, it's this:

Life by the inch is a cinch,
While life by the yard is hard."

Maybe there's something in that for us who are tempted to be goal-oriented and success-minded. We can learn to seize each day for its uniqueness, its opportunities, its possibilities. For today is all any of us has.

Anna has a motto over the washing machine:

> Yesterday is a cancelled cheque.
> Tomorrow is a promissory note.
> Today is cash for Christ.

Didn't Jesus say, "Don't worry about tomorrow"? Did he not teach us to pray, "Give us each day our daily bread" (Luke 11:3 RSV)? Remember what he said of himself, "I must work the works of him that sent me, while it is day" (John 9:4).

God has ordained our lives not to be lived all at once but in small units called days, and one at a time. If we desire to live today in Christ, if today we will experience God's love invading us, if we use the hours of this single day for showing that in some way his Kingdom is come in us, if we engage ourselves today in ministering to the needs of others, then we will bear witness to the power of these great words, "This is the day which the Lord has made; I will rejoice and be glad in it." Take today! It is God's gift, his unique gift to you.

Take Confidence

In my childhood home, in addition to the family there were two elderly people. One was my grandmother, and the other "Uncle" Crossley. For many years he had been a partner with my grandfather in evangelistic work in Canada and, being a bachelor, made his home with the Hunters. So we counted him always as part of the family. He belonged.

My mother often told me not to go in his bedroom which was on the third floor of our spacious house. But my childish curiosity frequently got the best of me, and when I thought it was safe I would tiptoe into his private domain. There I could look over his things and finger some of the artifacts of his many years, for he was well into his eighties.

What impressed me most, however, was a motto he kept over his bed. I read it every time I came in and often thought about it between times. It was simply those ancient words from Isaiah, "Thou wilt keep him in perfect peace, whose mind is stayed on thee: because he trusteth in thee" (Isa. 26:3). I memorized that, and although I didn't know quite what it meant, I somehow felt that it was a guiding light for him.

All this comes back to me now, no longer as a prettily decorated wall plaque but rather as a crucial necessity for our age. I recalled those words recently as I was reading an article with the title "The Traitor Inside." It is a discussion of our inability to cope with conditions of the seventies. The writer calls this "anxiety neurosis" and says that it results from the social and economic stress of our time. People are apprehensive. There is a mood of uncertainty in the land. Some of the old landmarks have been removed, and everything seems subject to change. Inflation and unemployment, violence and threat of war, are the daily fare offered on almost every newspaper's front page. No wonder people complain of sleeplessness, stomach distress, migrain, and even nightmares. The phrase *age of anxiety* is now a cliché. Writer Albert Camus calls ours "the century of fear." We suffer from loss of confidence.

But what is the root of this malady that frays the nerves, wears down the human spirit, and sets the mind in turmoil? Rollo May says simply it is anxiety, that threat to the self, the unsettled and unsettling sense, and the menacing thought of possible nothingness, emptiness, pointlessness. He writes that anxiety differs from fear in that fear has an object. But anxiety is like a fog. It is there yet impossible to touch or hold or push away.

The playwright Tennessee Williams says:

> Whether or not we admit it, we are all haunted by a truly awful sense of impermanence. . . . I have always had a particularly keen sense of this at New York cocktail parties and perhaps that is why I drink the martinis almost as fast as I can snatch them from the tray. Fear and evasion are two little beasts that chase each other's tails in the revolving wire cage of our nervous world.

Theologian Paul Tillich says that the basic source of anxiety is "the fear that the being which is 'I' will cease to be, that death will annihilate us."

Dr. Carl Michalson in his book *Faith for Personal Crises*

declares that "anxiety is the result of not knowing who you really are and to whom you really belong."

Surely related to these is the sense of purposelessness and meaninglessness, so widespread today. One of the saddest events of our time concerns Patricia Hearst, that young girl from one of America's foremost families, raised in wealth, culture, and with every door open for education, travel, and personal fulfillment. But she chucked it all and joined the Symbionese Liberation Army. Why? She said, "I was sick of the middle-class life I was leading. The SLA members seemed to have some purpose to their lives." Anxiety grows in the soil of purposelessness.

Added to these are the thoughts that come to us because of our explorations into space. The idea of an empty, endless universe, marked only by dead planets as barren as the moon and exploding into ever-increasing immensity, is enough to blow our minds. Is it for this reason that scientists are so bent on trying to discover life on other planets? Perhaps we think that if we were to find the slightest evidence of life "out there," we wouldn't feel so absolutely alone down here.

There is a play entitled *Dream of a World Without God*. A man is depicted who dreams that he awakens in a cemetery and finds himself in a world in which there is no God. Into the scene comes Christ. The voice of one recently expired asks, "Christ, is there no God?"

> "I have traversed the worlds, I have risen to the suns, with the milky-ways I have passed athwart the great waste spaces of the sky: there is no God. And I descended to where the very shadow cast by Being dies out and ends, and I gazed out into the gulf beyond, and cried, 'Father, where art Thou?' But answer there came none, save the eternal storm which rages on, controlled by none. . . .We

are orphans all, both I and ye. We have no Father. . . ."

Then he raised his eyes toward the nothingness and boundless void saying, "Oh, dead, dumb nothingness! Necessity endless and chill! Oh, mad, unreasoning Chance! when will ye dash this fabric into atoms, and me too? Every soul in this great corpse-trench of a universe is utterly alone! I am alone—O Father! Father! Where is that boundless breast of thine, that I may rest upon it? Alas! if every soul be its own creator and father, why shall it not be its own destroying angel too?"—from *Wit, Wisdom and Philosophy of Jean Paul Richter* (translation)

So in this dramatic form the author would have us contemplate a world without God, without an eternal Father, without life after death, without meaning, and without hope. Even a moment's exposure to such a possibility is enough to make us feel the surge of anxiety feelings rising up inside.

Just as the awfulness of this thought is about to overtake the dreamer and cast him into utter despair, he awakes. As the gloom dissolved like the horrible dream it was, and he saw God's world stretched out before him in all its glory, his soul "wept for joy."

If we were to make two lists under five headings, to compare the outcome of nihilistic thought to that of faith, it would probably come out something like this:

NIHILISM	*FAITH*
WHAT IT IS	
nothingness	historical event (God was in Christ)
empty space	experience (my own)
PERSONAL REACTION	
ultimately alone	God knows and loves me
life is meaningless	life has significance and purpose

pointless living	personal goal
hopelessness	anticipation of new things
boredom	excitement
fear	courage
worry	peace
fretting	ease
dullness	zest for living
anxiety	confidence

VALUES

no ultimate values	responsibility and accountability to the creator God
everything is relative	God is God; he is the Absolute
flesh is god	stewardship of the body and of material possessions
material possessions are first importance	
no conscience	sensitivity to right and wrong

RELATIONSHIPS

other people get in the way	other people are considered brothers and sisters
scheme to outdo others	cooperate for the good of all
competition (win at any price)	caring
exploitation (no scruples)	accountable for others' welfare

RESULTS

dread	exhilaration
gloom	hunger for more life
ultimate defeat	security
despair	hopefulness

illness	health
potential suicide	abundant life
feel trapped in vicious circle of existence	free to grow

The Bible confidently assures us of God's care and that "in returning and rest shall ye be saved: in quietness and in confidence shall be your strength" (Isa. 30:15). To keep the mind stayed on the God who is and who cares and who controls is to know "perfect peace."

But perhaps our greatest source of confidence comes from Jesus' words in Luke 12. He urges his disciples not to worry about food or clothing, the very basics of life. He points to the birds, the flowers, and the grasses, all of which are maintained by God. Then he turns to the disciples and says bluntly, "But you have a Father." The birds have God, but "you have a Father." It's as if he is saying, "How come you didn't know that?" Or, "Perhaps you have forgotten." But this is the most important fact of all facts, and it has within it the secret of confidence.

Here, to my mind, is the cause and basic cure for anxiety as well as the key to our ability to live confidently in a threatening world. We have a Father! When we forget that fact we become vulnerable to a host of devilish emotions, thoughts, and moods, chief of which is a growing and unnerving anxiety. This little poem by Elizabeth Chaney expresses it simply and accurately:

> Said the Robin to the Sparrow:
> "I should really like to know
> Why these anxious human beings
> Rush about and worry so."
>
> Said the Sparrow to the Robin:
> "Friend, I think that it must be

That they have no heavenly Father
Such as cares for you and me."

Jesus' characteristic word for God is *Father*. Right from his first teachings of the Sermon on the Mount he talks about his Father, and when he taught them to pray he told them to say "our Father." In that most intimate conversation recorded in John 14, Jesus uses the term *Father* no less than 22 times climaxing his thought with the statement, "Anyone who has seen me has seen the Father" (v. 9 NEB).

As Father, God is our provider, giving us whatever we ask in the name of Christ. More than that, he is our divine Lover, waiting with amazing patience for us to come home so that he can deluge us with his gracious gifts. This Father will go so far as to lay down his own life for the sake of his children.

One of the most poignant passages in the Bible is the account of David's grief over the death of his son Absalom.

> And the king was deeply moved, and went up to the chamber over the gate, and wept; and as he went, he said, "O my son Absalom, my son, my son Absalom! Would I had died instead of you, O Absalom, my son, my son!" (II Sam. 18:33 RSV)

Here is the feeling of fatherhood at its human best. Although Absalom fought against his father, I believe David would gladly have died in Absalom's stead.

A few years ago a certain Japanese industrialist committed suicide. He did so because his son had joined a rebel group with whom he had committed many crimes including several murders. Because he felt deeply involved through love for his son, this father took his own life and left a note which read, "With my death I offer apologies for crimes committed by my son. Do not accuse the other surviving members of my family."

Just so does a father feel for and with his son. But then how much more our Father God! Theologian Helmut Thielicke says in *Nihilism:*

> When a man sees the fact of Jesus Christ and it dawns on him that the universe is fatherly and that he is loved, he loses his fear. Not that all the oppressing, depressing powers are banished from his life. . . . But they can no longer compel him to gaze into the frightening abyss of meaninglessness and rob him of the peace that is assured him. [Otherwise] he is on a constant hunt for artificial ways of filling up his time. Anxiety is intolerable and therefore it must be constantly diverted. The more quiet things are, the more the yawning void appears and the more anxiety creeps in.

So it would seem that anxiety comes from not knowing this Father God who never gives up searching for us. We then rush around desperately trying substitutes to fill up the void, always frantically on the move, so that there will be no time left open to face the awful emptiness of our existence.

Confidence comes when, acknowledging God as Father, we allow him to find us, and then, knowing we have been found, living day by day with the constancy of his accepting love.

A minister friend of mine was walking one day through the aisles of a large department store. He noticed a group of people gathered around a small boy who was wailing his grief. Inquiring what was wrong, he was told that the lad was lost. He had come into the store with his father, but in the huge crowds they had become separated. The tearful boy had gone frantically up one stairs, onto an elevator, down to another floor, and then around the counters and was now fearful he might be lost forever. So he just sat down and cried.

My friend suggested to the others that he could handle the situation and turning to the boy said, "Now, don't cry," and he wiped away the tears. Then he added, "Do you see that high counter over there, the one directly in front of those elevators? Well, I'm going to set you right up there where you can be seen easily. Then we'll stick together; you just wait and see. I believe that in a very few minutes your dad will come off one of those elevators, and he'll spot you right away. Because while you've been running all over looking for him, I am sure he's been going from one floor to another looking for you. So if we just stay quietly in this one place, he'll come." The little fellow was comforted. Sure enough, it wasn't long before the man stepped off the elevator and had his little son in his arms.

In this manner God searches us out. Because God is, and because he is our Father, and because he is finally in control all the ultimates are intact. With shoulders back we can go forward with joy. It is his grace that takes the initiative to find us and when we are convinced of that fact, we can take the confidence that is his gift.

Take Your Time

Anna and I are good examples of people living at different speeds. I was brought up in a home where my father wanted things done immediately—sooner if possible. His most recurring phrase was "Hurry up!" much to the frequent consternation of my mother. Anna was raised in a more relaxed atmosphere in which things were done not by the clock but by the season. I was trained to keep a schedule, but her early years were marked by lived-out feelings. In my home things had to get done. In hers, moments were relished for their unique value.

All this came to a head at the Frankfurt, Germany, airport where we had been grounded for a couple of hours between flights. We were a long way from home; neither of us could speak the language, and I began to experience anxiety feelings. What would happen if we became separated in the crowd or if my wallet were stolen or if we didn't hear the message when our plane was called for boarding? So I was up tight. But Anna was completely relaxed and very much unconcerned.

After a while I did hear our flight called, and when I looked at where my wife had been sitting, there was only an empty seat. Where could she have gone? If she were in the women's room, how could I get her out of there? How long would she be? Did she hear our plane called? I knew she couldn't have gone on ahead, because I had the tickets. I was really upset.

However, as soon as the crowd began to thin out I spotted her. There she was in the outdoor restaurant, standing before her portable easel, paintbrush in hand, nonchalantly capturing a peaceful scene on canvas. Though in my haste I had to break up her idyllic mood for the sake of getting our flight, we still have the beautiful painting she did that day, and I treasure it.

Time means different things to different people. Some are forever saying, "I wish I had more time," while others have time on their hands. We do various things to time. We sometimes waste time, kill time, budget time, hurry to save time, or wait to put in time. Some people will fret over losing five minutes in the grocery check-out line, but then go home and sit for two hours of drivel on television. The Bible recounts the life of a man named Methuselah. He seems to hold the record for long life because he lived nine hundred sixty-nine years. But the only thing the account says about him beyond his achievement of such great age was "he died." All that time, and so little to show for it!

Time is life. It is a slice out of eternity. We cannot create it or buy it but only accept it. It is God's gift, for when he gave us life he also gave us time as the framework for our earthly existence. Time is our "living space" within which we can grow and work, doing what God assigns us in life and becoming the persons he intends us to be. Time also provides us with the challenge to come to terms with life itself, its crises, its choices, and its challenges. So time is grace, a gift from God.

Our time is spaced out over nonreturnable days. It isn't given all at once but in manageable units. If we misuse a day it cannot be done over. Each day is to be lived out in its unique possibilities. Again I recall my wife's motto: Yesterday is a cancelled cheque. Tomorrow is a promissory note. Today is cash for Christ.

How irreversible and fast moving time is! This fact comes home to me when we go to our summer cottage which now spans five generations of Hunters. About 1895 my grandfather bought two islands in the Muskoka Lake district of Ontario. Those were the days when land sold for one dollar an acre. And while we have only the small one now in our possession, it has been a family center where the clan gathers every summer. The cottage is old-fashioned, spacious, and designed for gracious living. Many of the furnishings are antiquated, and there are shelves upon shelves of old books, old papers, and much bric-a-brac. There are many large, faded pictures and portraits in ornamental frames. Occasionally I'll pick up a book written a hundred years ago and find hidden among the yellowed papers some fragile, folded paper which is handwritten, a letter sent by somebody to somebody else, giving details of how many pails of blueberries were picked or how many fish were caught and the size of the biggest. After reading such a note, I gently fold it up and reverently put it back. And then I breathe a hope that nobody in the future will destroy it so that it might continue to enable people to dip back momentarily into the past and feel as I do and sense the brevity of life.

The years go swifter as we get older. I can remember my dad telling me when I was a child that his father came to the cottage area "t-h-i-r-t-y years ago," and it sounded to me like an eternity. How could anybody have that much history? But how well I know it now!

Jesus lived on earth only thirty-three years. He had a

perfect sense of timing. Among his first recorded words are, "The time has come; the kingdom of God is upon you; repent, and believe the Gospel" (Mark 1:15 NEB). Repeatedly in his teachings he referred to the right time. He said, "My time is not yet come" (John 7:8 NEB). "Father, the hour has come," "I must work the works of him that sent me, while it is day; the night cometh when no man can work" (John 17:1 RSV; 9:4). Paul expressed the same kind of sensitivity when he wrote, "When the fulness of the time was come, God sent forth his Son" (Gal. 4:4).

To realize that time is life and that both are gifts from God is to know how to use time and, in turn, how to appropriate its stream of gifts. I saw a wall plaque that read, "Ve git too soon olde and too late schmart!" True, but God is waiting for us to smarten up so that we understand what the days and months and years all add up to. And what else but to know God, to accept his grace, to reflect his love, and to help others know the same?

Life is not only to be measured in days but in time stages, and each stage is unique for its own opportunity and possibility. Youth feels the exhilaration of facing the future. Middle age feels the maturing process of bearing responsibility. Old age feels the joy of reflection and the understanding that comes with the accumulated wisdom of the years.

Time magazine ran a cover story on the latest female beauties: the newest movie starlets, models, cover girls, ballet dancers. They are beautiful and they are young. But they are *only* young. As I read the article I was made aware that we have developed a youth culture that is relatively new in history, and we have put supreme value on youthful looks and figure. Many people have become victims of this emphasis and spend a great deal of time pining over lost youth.

Within the gift of time, each stage of life has its special if sometimes hidden gift. People who realize this become more beautiful and more handsome as they get older. The passing years do not bring loss but gain. Why try to rub out the signs of the years? We can "glory in the gray" and "rejoice in our wrinkles," because time writes character on the countenance, and we begin to reflect the faith, hope, and love that are in us.

If time is a gift from God, then surely he gave us all we need to do, all that he intends us to do. For some years as I walked to my work in the morning, I would notice that there were two trees at the end of our street, one a tall spruce and the other a willow. The spruce stood straight and clear against the morning sky with definite shape and upward growth. The willow was a blur. It had no definition, no visible trunk, no clear lines and pointed in no one direction. As I went along contemplating those trees I would say to myself, "Gordon Hunter, God is giving you a new day! The result of how you use it is illustrated by the spruce or the willow. It can be a day of purpose, of clear goals and can carry a definite message. Or it can be just a clutter of unrelated happenings and unproductive activities. Which shall it be?" Those two trees continue to exist vividly in my memory and frequently challenge me at the beginning of my day. Somebody said, "Today is the first day of the rest of your life." This is just another way of saying what the Bible means in the words: "It is high time to awake out of sleep . . . The night is far spent, the day is at hand" (Rom. 13:11). "Now is the accepted time; . . . now is the day of salvation" (II Cor. 6:2).

The Bible uses a very special word for this type of opportune time. It is called *kairos*. Time is given more than a simple quantitative measurement, a qualitative dimension. Occasions of kairos are unforgettable. They are times of supreme happiness or profound sorrow or else important turning points in making crucial decisions. When kairos comes we may say something like "Time stood still" and yet not be able to remember precisely how long the experience lasted. We remember it as a time of great intensity, total absorption, and insight.

The writer of Ecclesiastes says, "To every thing there is a season, and a time to every purpose under the heaven: A time to be born, and a time to die; a time to plant, and a time to pluck up that which is planted; . . . a time to weep, and a time to mourn, and a time to dance; . . . a time to keep silence, and a time to speak" (3:1-7). To recognize these times is to be aware of kairos.

Shakespeare put it in these awesome words in *Julius Caesar:*

> There is a tide in the affairs of men,
> Which, taken at the flood, leads on to fortune;
> Omitted, all the voyage of their life
> Is bound in shallows and in miseries.

Obedience requires not only that we recognize kairos but that we respond to it, discern its meaning, take advantage of it, use it to its potential. An illustration of what I mean is that moment our family experienced when our pet rabbit was killed, probably by a fox or raccoon. We had had him for two years, and he was very special, beautiful with thick, bluish gray fur. Very appropriately, our two girls called him Blueberry.

Marjorie, who was eleven, took extra special care of him, making sure he got his water, pellets, and cabbage every morning and, with the help of her younger sister, Angela, seeing that his cage was properly cleaned out every Saturday morning. So we gave him lots of love, and we assumed he felt the same way toward us. Anyway, one morning we looked out, and by the disturbance of the cage and the yard we knew that something terrible had happened. Then we learned the gruesome facts.

The first reaction of our girls was as you might expect; a mixture of terror, rage, and tears, in the midst of which Anna and I did our best to comfort, soothe, and sympathize. Then it struck me: this is kairos! We can learn something about nature and its built-in cruelties and more, about violence in the world and man's inhumanity to man. We can learn how God relates to all this and what the Bible means when it indicates that when his Kingdom comes in its fullness, nature also will be redeemed with mankind so that "the wolf also shall dwell with the lamb, and the leopard shall lie down with the kid; and the calf and the young lion and the fatling together. . . . They shall not hurt nor destroy: . . . for the earth shall be full of the knowledge of the Lord, as the waters cover the sea" (Isa. 11:6, 9). Meanwhile, all of nature groans, as Paul said. It groans for a better day, for reconciliation, peace, and love.

At first I wondered how an eleven-year-old girl would take my attempt to interpret the event, especially since she was still in a state of semishock. Would it only make matters worse? Would she reject what I might say as being no help at all? She wanted her bunny back.

With some fear I approached the issue, and to my

surprise she was fascinated by what I said in trying to interpret the sad event. She wanted to hear more. It seemed to help her put things in perspective. With this understanding she was better able to accept what had happened and to cope with her own feelings. Yes, it surely turned out to be a kairos.

Suppose we think of life as a drama and ourselves as actors playing our part on stage. All of a sudden the cue comes, and somebody says to us, "You're on!" This is the moment for us to speak, to do our thing, to play our part. The drama is God's. History is his story. If God is the author, Jesus Christ is the director, and the Holy Spirit is the prompter.

The drama begins with Act 1: "In the beginning God created the heavens and the earth" (Gen. 1:1 RSV). Act 2 marks the entrance of the author, God, into the drama in the person of Jesus Christ. "The Word was made flesh, and dwelt amongst us" (John 1:14). Act 3 begins when Christ returns. Our time is when we are working out or acting out the implications of Christ's ministry on earth. All who are aware of this divine drama have a part to play, unique, individual, and important. The part each person plays is his or her individual drama, undertaken with joy in the realization that Christ is Lord of our time.

Those unaware of the drama fritter away their time off stage, or they may be sitting in the audience thinking that the only purpose of life is to be entertained. Somehow if life for them is to be meaningful, they must come to know that there is a drama being worked out, and they have a vital part to play in it. Our own sense of involvement may, in turn, be their cue.

So God gives us this precious thing called time. It is our lifespan. It is a sacred and glorious trust. If we are sensitive, we will hear his words, "You're on!" We will recognize our kairos, and we will move onstage and play out our unique part. Nobody can do it for us. And when the curtain comes down we will have fulfilled in some measure the meaning of our time on earth.

The Privilege of Being Accepted

I'm O.K.–You're O.K., the popular book on transactional analysis, is full of helpful suggestions, creative ideas, and understanding of human nature as well as some valuable techniques on dealing with personal problems.

It is easy to understand why this has been one of the most widely read books of the decade. Hardly was it off the press when sales zoomed. Churches have been using it, and scores of courses on the general teaching of the book are offered in a variety of settings. The author, Thomas Harris, has become such a speaker in demand that since the publication of the book, which was written out from his own psychiatric practice, he has had to give up private work to become almost a full-time traveler and lecturer.

Why is it so popular? Well, in addition to being well written, most people find it easy to read and understand. It is a popular guide to being a happier person, without all the psychological terminology which has put the whole subject quite out of the reach of ordinary people.

But those are only surface reasons. A more important factor, I believe, is the book's theme and title. The chapters are all about how to accept yourself and others. Here is an easy-to-apply technique to come to like yourself and hence live happily with yourself. It shows how a person can confidently say, "I'm OK" and, in addition, learn to say honestly to others, "You're OK."

This confronts head on, one of the deepest, most

widespread problems of many people: the feeling of being personally rejected. Few things can happen to us that are potentially more devastating than this debilitating experience. We can take many blows to body or mind. We can sustain physical suffering, disappointment, and shock. But the hardest blow of all is to feel unliked, unwanted, not accepted.

People may reject us. We may feel rejected by God or perhaps even reject ourselves. This can happen in many ways. For instance, imagine a man for many years working diligently in an office or factory, putting in long hours, and striving for honesty, dignity, and competence in his work. He is suddenly told one morning that he is being replaced by a machine. Rejection! Or, a teen-ager suddenly packs up his bags and his books, moves out, and, without any sense of gratitude, leaves a note for his parents in which he simply says, "I don't need you anymore." Those parents know the pain of rejection.

Here is an individual who strives for years against inner moral conflict. He gradually becomes more and more undisciplined, bad-tempered, perhaps alcoholic. Finally he gives up the effort and concludes, "I'm just no good." Such self-rejection is often the prelude to suicide.

Because of this fear, people will go to great lengths to make themselves acceptable. This motive lies back of a good deal of social conformity. We run with the group because we want our peers to think well of us. Many people drink socially, not because they want to, but because they are afraid to do otherwise, for that would mean nonconformity. Advertisers know this human trait and exploit it. More and more people let themselves go into debt, buying things they don't need and may not want, all for the sake of conformity, social approval, acceptance.

So in the face of this, along came the book with the intriguing title *I'm O.K.–You're O.K.* It shocks us into the awareness of a new possibility. It is what all of us long to say and believe but perhaps do not dare. So, no wonder it is a best seller! No wonder churches are using it! It seems to be expressing in contemporary terms something of the good news of the gospel of Jesus Christ. A cartoon I saw recently shows a minister preaching from a high pulpit and with great, dramatic gestures declaring to the congregation, "And so I say unto you, 'I'm OK, you're OK!'" The people reply in unison, "Amen, brother! You're OK and we're OK!" Everybody feels that everything is OK, and that's great so far as it goes.

The trouble is, words by themselves cannot create genuine OK feelings. Much of this popular approach is just surface treatment. I doubt that I could be made to feel totally acceptable, at least for very long, just because some other person may slap me on the back and say, "You're OK."

A boy came home from school with a bad report card. He had done much below his usual average on a recent set of tests. His mother tried to console him and said, "Oh, well, everybody fails occasionally, and you'll be all right in time." But he couldn't take it. Turning to his mother he said, "Mom, I made a mess of those tests; so why not both of us admit it?" This young man had such guilty feelings about his poor performance that soothing words—no matter how well intentioned by his loving mother—could not really console.

Human guilt, human sin, human fear, human inferiority feelings go much deeper than any easy-going, buck-up, slap-me-on-the-back treatment will overcome. While modern psychology says "accept yourself," a thoughtful person might reply, "Great! But how can I accept an unacceptable self?"

An answer may be suggested in the story of the young fellow who came one day into a small store and asked to use the telephone. The man behind the counter gave permission and could not help overhearing the conversation. The lad had dialed someone who obviously was a very important person; he had to go through three secretaries to reach his party.

"Sir, do you want a boy to work for you, to shovel your snow, to cut your grass in the summer, and generally to clean up your grounds?" he asked.

The answer, "No, I have a boy."

He pressed further, "And you are satisfied with him?"

"Oh, yes," came the reply, "I'm more than satisfied, in fact he is doing a great job."

"All right," he said with satisfaction, and hung up.

The storekeeper, feeling for the lad said, "Sorry, you didn't get the job." The young fellow looked startled and replied, "Oh, don't worry. I have a job. You see, I'm the boy who works for that man, and I was just checking up on myself."

He went to the ultimate authority and got it straight from the top, "You're doing OK." If we want to be ultimately, authoritatively, absolutely, unequivocally convinced that we're OK, we must go to the top too, to the highest authority, to God himself. Nothing less will do.

Paul said, "If God be for us, who can be against us?" (Rom. 8:31). We could restate these words, "If God says we're OK, who can say we're not OK?" On the other hand, we could turn the idea around and say that if we don't hear God telling us we're OK, no number of humans no matter how competent could persuade us of the fact.

Suppose we make up our minds once and for all that God is for us. Many people just can't believe that because it seems too good to be true. They picture God as some almighty judge who is waiting to fault them here and there and then condemn. Well, there is judgment in life, unavoidably so, but God is more than judge.

A little girl was writing a composition on the family. "God made parents," she said, "to keep saying 'no' to children." It is easy to see why some children conclude that parents are against them. They may have been subjected to a constant barrage of criticism, been overly corrected, unduly judged, forever compared to others, and bitterly scolded. If we have inadequate knowlege or experience of God or if we feel always guilty before him, we won't likely think of him as being very accepting.

Yet the good news of the gospel is that God is for us, in favor of us. He believes in us, he is patient with us, he wants always only the best for us. Remember that old stalwart Job? He felt totally rejected. Sitting on a pile of ashes outside the city gate, he has lost everything he had. From being a man of affluence and respect, he is reduced to poverty, suffering, humiliation. Three friends come to tell him in so many words that God has rejected him, and that's the only sensible reason for his desperate condition. But Job won't buy that idea. He admits that he doesn't know what God is up to most of the time but in a great burst of faith declares, "I know that my Vindicator lives." Despite all the evidence to the contrary, he was sure God was for him, and some day he'd understand what's been going on. He firmly believed that God was good.

An example of personal conviction is George

McGovern who ran as a candidate for the presidency of the United States. He is a committed Christian. On election night as the returns were coming in, he went to bed at 7:30 and slept until 9:00. Only an inwardly confident person could do that. Then as he checked results, it became clearer by the hour that he would be defeated. It is natural to think that this would result in a sense of personal rejection, especially since the victory of his opponent was so overwhelming. But McGovern said, "I know there's going to be a lot of talk about how humiliating my defeat was. It won't bother me. I feel quite secure in my own person. I don't regard my loss so much as a personal rejection as a rejection of the things I stood for. I have been at peace with myself. You see, I wasn't running for personal advancement. I was running for a cause." Even if the majority of a whole nation rejects you, you are still not really rejected if you have confidence in something bigger and beyond yourself.

The final proof of God's acceptance, Paul says, is God's sparing not his own Son but giving him up for us all! The Cross is God's way of saying to us, "You're OK, I accept you, no matter who you are or what you've done." If we are once convinced of that fact, then we must accept ourselves, for, as one man put it, "If the Divine Craftsman made you, you'd better not despise the product."

God is for us, not because he glosses over the meanness and selfishness of our prideful nature. Acceptance is not necessarily approval. He accepts us because we are his, provided we have given ourselves over to him. All the while he may disapprove of what we do. No amount of patting ourselves on the back and saying "I'm OK" can really help, because in our more sober moments we sometimes catch a glimpse of our real selves, our unloving attitudes, our childish reactions, our mixed-up motives, and dishonesty in many of our offhanded statements. God sees through all this pretense even though we may keep trying to persuade ourselves that we're OK.

Paul says, "If God be for us, who can be against us?" (Rom. 8:31). He lists some human adversities: tribulation, distress, persecution, famine, nakedness, peril, sword. He rules out all these with one resounding no! He goes further, "In all these things"—note that, not "in spite of all these things"—"in all these things we are more than conquerors through him that loved us" (Rom. 8:37).

I have been in groups in which people played this game. Two or three persons are given identical items of paper, scissors, paste, and a few other things, and then instructed to make something, such as a lady's hat. Well, what they usually come up with is highly amusing and provides a good many laughs as the imaginative designers put their outlandish creations on their heads and parade around. But quite often, after the laughs are done with, somebody comes up with a hat that is truly beautiful, a piece of art, exhibiting the work of a talented person.

Living is something like this game. Nobody is given the choice of the basic elements: where she is born or when, to what family she may be given, how many talents she will possess, or what opportunities may be presented. The basics of life are all given. But what makes the dramatic difference is what we do with these givens. If, deep down, we feel we are not accepted, then we may not even think it worth the effort to be anybody or to accomplish anything. But, if we know for sure that we are accepted, then no matter how few nor how inadequate are the basics, we will create something good and useful.

A boy was stricken with paralysis before he was ten. He lost seven years of schooling. His body was dwarfed and deformed. He was only an eighty-seven-pound cripple. But when he was allowed to study again he was determined to make up for lost time. Could he enter sports? It seemed impossible. He couldn't even walk. But he trained as the coxswain of the rowing crew, who is responsible for steering and shouting commands. With a larger than usual megaphone because of his weak voice and with a special steering apparatus because of his crippled arm, time and again he brought his team to victory. He had learned to accept himself, to make the most of what he'd been given. Think of his many possible alternative responses: rebellion, despair, self-pity, apathy, uselessness. He rejected all that. There were many things about his frail body that were not OK, but he himself was very much OK.

So God doesn't merely give us a pat on the back. He does something that causes deep suffering to himself but that demonstrates his amazing love for us. If there were no cross, I would have no right, in fact I would have no grounds, to say "I'm OK" or "You're OK." That would be cheap grace. It does little ultimate good to come to a person whose spirits are down, slap him on the back glibly, and say, "Buck up." That's not good news and may lead to even deeper despair.

It is God himself who says, "You're OK." He has made us OK by his suffering love. Hence, when we've really heard this good news and accepted it and truly believed it, then we can confidently and with full assurance say, "I *am* OK." The world may knock the stuffing out of us. Life may kick us unmercifully. Even those nearest and dearest may seem at times to reject us. But God's message keeps coming through, "You're OK."

This is not the end of the gospel but its beginning, not a stage we finally reach but our starting point. Self-acceptance leads to acceptance of others.

Not being something we obtain for ourselves, all this is a gift and therefore the result of grace. "If God be for us, who can be against us?" Christians live always under the sense of the privilege of being constantly and repeatedly accepted. God says to each of us, "You're OK because I've made you OK."

Don't Be Afraid to Ask for More

A reporter went to Paris to interview the duchess of Windsor. He described her as a bored, lonely, and sometimes ailing woman. She still goes the weary round of clotheries, hairdressers, and restaurants but spends much of her time alone, reading detective novels. "Life is a bombshell," she says. "I no longer understand it or like it. It is full of violence and horror." She has few friends and is hard put to gather enough for a tea party.

When the duke died in 1972 he made no bequests to church, charity, family, or favorite servants. His private possessions remain just as he left them or last used them. His shirts are still stacked in his drawers, his suits hanging in the closet, his toilet articles exactly in place, and his desk ready for instant use. Even paper clips and pipe cleaners are handy, and his many photographs of the duchess stand on his mantel and bookcases, just as he left them. Every night, according to her servants, the duchess goes into his room and says, "Good night, David."

She continues to live in a villa just outside Paris and manages with a staff of seventeen. "Thunderstorms bother me, and I don't like going up in planes," she says. Around the property there is a high spiked fence. The gate is under constant guard, and there is an electronic alarm system attached to every window. A special patrol keeps watch outside. She has a "hot line" to the local police station, and special security agents are always on call. She no longer takes sleeping pills, because she wants to remain alert. Often in the night she will look out the window just to check to see if the guards are on duty. She sleeps with the duke's pistol at her side.

What a pathetic way to live! Seeming to have little interest in events or people she exists in a private world of her own, marked by fear, sorrow, and dread. Wallowing in her wealth one may ask, "But to what purpose?" To be sure, she has her memories, but many of these are bitter and sad.

Life for her could be so much more. What if she were to give herself to some important project, such as offering to put a new heart machine in a hospital in India or to assist in the fantastic work of Sister Teresa in Calcutta? What if she were to underwrite the expenses of educating a young man or woman from Nairobi or were to finance a home for retarded children under Jean Vanier's program? The needs are so great, and the ways to help so obvious! Yet here is a person who remains shut up within herself. Is it any wonder life for her is boring, dull, sad, and futile?

Countless people live more or less like the duchess while God is offering so much more. The Bible states this divine offer in many ways. "For with thee is the fountain of life" (Ps. 36:9). "My cup runs over" (Ps. 23:5 NEB). "How precious also are thy thoughts unto me, O God! how great is the sum of them! If I should count them, they are more . . . than the sand: when I awake, I am still with thee" (Ps. 139:17–18). Jesus said, "I am come that they might have life, and . . . have it more abundantly" (John 10:10). "If God so clothe the grass, . . . shall he not much more clothe you?" "Is not the life more than meat, and the body than raiment?" (Matt. 6:30, 25). "If you, then, bad as you are, know how to give your children what is good . . . , how much more will your heavenly Father give good things to those who ask him!'' (Matt. 7:11 NEB). Paul said, "We are more than conquerors through him who loved us" (Rom. 8:37 RSV).

God is our Father who always wants to give more. His goodness is beyond our dreams, his mercy beyond our imagination, his grace beyond our needs, and his generosity beyond our highest expectancy.

The idea of more usually comes as real good news. Do you remember when you were just a child, and your mother (the best cook in all the world) brought on your favorite dessert? She always made good puddings and cakes, but this one was her extra-special delight. Your eyes lighted up when you saw it coming, and your mouth watered in anticipation of tasting that goodness. But when you took your last spoonful it was gone! You scraped the dish, and when you felt no one was looking you perhaps licked it as well. It was then that your mother brought good news. "I didn't serve it all," she said. "There's more!"

So I believe God is constantly saying to us even in our most delightful moments when life is so good we've licked our plate and smacked our lips, "There's more!"

In the tale of Jonathan Livingston Seagull (the little book that swept the country some years ago) there is a climactic ending. Fletcher, one of Jonathan's pupils, is gradually learning to fly, to really fly with freedom, and is tingling with the sense of the potential and possibilities still locked up with him. It is then he remembers learning a phrase from his instructor, "No limits!"

Our tendency is to put boundaries around ourselves and to accept all those limitations which life itself imposes. Eating, working, playing, sleeping, absorb so much of our time and energy that we are tempted to believe that life is only those things. We begin to think we are more than limited, we're trapped! But God always wants to break through our limitations and show us his "more": more joy, more health, more satisfaction, more fulfillment. If we want it, it's ours. If we take Christ seriously when he said "I came that you might have life more abundantly," then we'll know these possibilities are available.

This is especially important in these times of growing shortages. There is starvation in our world, horrible, repulsive starvation. And yet we are told there is enough food for everybody when we are ready to transport it from the location of surplus to the places of greatest need. To accomplish this, the requirement is not merely for ships and planes so much as for the will to do it and a caring heart for motivation. If we go to war over shortages of oil or food, we will be like a family quarreling over the dinner table. The result will be loss and ruin for everybody. But God's "more" in terms of his resources can be ours when we are willing to share, to admit that the world is made up of brothers in one family around one Father's table.

Ours is a consumer society, dedicated to producing more so we can sell more in order to earn more so that we can spend more. It is a vicious circle. To keep this system going faster all the time, new wants must be created as old wants are manufactured. Advertising makes us dissatisfied so we buy that product. Someone has defined advertising as "persuading people who don't know to spend money they don't have to buy things they don't need to impress people they don't like."

Perhaps our shortages add up to God's judgment on

our whole system. And the faster we are willing to move from competition toward cooperation, the faster everybody can have his "more."

A couple whom we have known for years recently attended a marriage-encounter course given in a Roman Catholic retreat center. When I first heard of their going I wondered if they had some trouble in their marriage about which the rest of us knew nothing. But when they showed us the brochure it was made quite plain that this course was not for marriages that were having trouble. It was designed for good marriages that could be made better. And our friends testified how they had learned higher levels of communication with each other and experienced new depths of listening. So even to "good marriages" there comes this wonderful news that there is much more happiness possible.

Once in a while we have an experience of ecstasy that leaves us at a loss for words to express our joy. Well, I happen to believe that those peak experiences, life's greatest joys and highest pleasures which are too big for our minds to grasp or our hearts to express, are given to us as a taste of God's "more" which he has in store for us. Paul expressed it, "What no one ever saw or heard, what no one ever thought could happen, is the very thing God prepared for those who love him" (I Cor. 2:9 TEV).

The hymn by Edward Henry Bickersteth says:

> A joy no language measures,
> A fountain brimming o'er,
> An endless flow of pleasures,
> An ocean without shore.

Rufus Jones was a well-known Quaker leader, writer, teacher, and preacher. He was in Europe when he received word that his son, his only son, was desperately ill. Immediately he made his way home to America but not in time to see his boy before he died, the victim of leukemia.

The man's sorrow was heavy. The burden of his great loss remained with him the rest of his life. But it was not a grieving unto despair, for he was a man of shining faith and expressed it in this unforgettable sentence: "Where there is so much love, there must be more." More love, more life. There is always more to come, more to be given, more to be received, more to be known, more to be experienced, more of everything—not just for the future but now.

"As bad as you are, you know how to give good things to your children. How much more, then, will your Father in heaven give good things to those who ask him!" So don't be afraid to ask for more, God's more for you!